THE SLANDER OF NOD
Waking Up Asleep

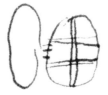

Anthony D. Sinner

Introduction

I tell my mother that the reason her six children became who they became is in no small part due to one thing: she subscribed to *The New Yorker* magazine. The most recent issue was always on the coffee table, ready to indoctrinate us. We discovered that the cartoons were sometimes very funny, the cosmopolitan opinions maybe weren't so different from ours, and having an intense interest in the arts seemed to be perfectly acceptable. Who knew?

I grew up in the rural Midwest in the 1960s and 70s buoyed by three generations of farmers on both sides of my family. The land under my young feet was rich and black and as flat as the ocean. It made an impression on my soul. The endless tilled soil, the expansive sky, the persistent winds, the unrelenting cold winters, the summers of heat and harvest – it all left me with an appreciation of the beauty of austerity.

Maybe the natural simplicity of this place is what attracted my eccentric ancestors to it long ago. From what I can gather, some of them were people who would rather have been left alone than entertained, whose creativity would have been able to fill the expansive empty gaps in space and time. Perhaps, my vivid dream life can be attributed in some way to that same fertile imagination.

The short dream stories and quick illustrations that follow were originally put down on the pages of a blank book. They appear here in the chronological order in which they were first written on those pages, with a few exceptions. The original writings have been edited for readability and the names of most of the real people encountered in the dreams have been changed. Otherwise, the events themselves have been preserved as lived. Episodes not remembered clearly are characterized that way or omitted altogether.

This little book tells of a life lived asleep, landscapes walked, people encountered, conversations had, and the efforts to make sense of it all. Sometimes I knew I was dreaming. One time I thought I had already woken up. Like everyone who dreams, I was simply living through events that weren't actually occurring, usually in places that didn't actually exist.

Some of my dream experiences stay with me. Singular, poignant, otherworldly, even life-changing, they have become part of my personal history, landmarks on a shifting horizon. But most of my dream experiences remain amorphous. Only when written down did they take on persistence and clarity, like hooked fish finally dragged from muddy waters.

What you can read in the following pages is what I witnessed and faithfully recorded. In my opinion, however, none of it really happened.

– Anthony D. Sinner, 2021

Contents

Waking Up

I woke up to a pleasant summer morning, the low sun casting long shadows across the patio. With a deep breath and a stretch I sat up. I had spent the night in a sleeping bag on top of the picnic table in the back yard of my boyhood home. Bundling the bedding under my arm, I got down from my plywood perch, walked through the rear garage door and proceeded into the house. As I rearranged my misappropriated mop of hair I greeted my mother in the kitchen and began to look for some breakfast. Then, like a bolt of lightning, I woke up again, in bed in my dorm room.

dreamed at college, circa 1980, written 12/1/93

This dream-incident has stuck with me and influenced my view of the nature of reality.

Parking in Paris

I was living in Paris in an apartment overlooking the Champs Élysées. I found myself in a small car parked near a curb. A traffic official was asking me to move. There had been mention of some concern about parking on the street outside my apartment because of the bus stop there. I looked out the passenger's side door and found that, under the leaves and debris, the curb was indeed painted yellow. So, I began to move my car. I remembered reading earlier that the city had hired a four-piece brass band to play incidental music while parking law violators were moving their cars, presumably to mock them. I did not hear any music or see any band.

A bit later in a grassy park in my neighborhood I was playing ball with a couple of friends. The grass was quite brown and the hedge skirting the play field was nearly bare. We were dressed in warm coats and there was a chill in the clear, sunny air. One of my friends, Tom, was obese yet athletic. The other was actor Leonard Nimoy. We were playing with a pink spongy football, making flashy passes, no-lookers, behind-the-backers, etc. Many of my passes were incompetent in one way or another, but I felt it was still understood that I was the best athlete among us. I made one last, long throw, from one end of the field to the other, after which the three of us met in the middle and began to walk off. This is when I noticed that my companions heads had been completely obscured by giant clover leaves and stems, sprouting from the collars of their jackets.

dreamed late March 8, or the early March 9, 1993

ANTHONY D. SINNER

Jet Plane

There we were, in confrontation: the unwelcome Americans on one side and the khaki-clad middle-easterners on the other. We Americans were positioned on a dome-topped military tank, some of us waist-deep in turret. Our counterparts were dark-haired and scruffy-bearded, dressed in dusty, worn uniforms, crumpled of cap and rolled-up of sleeve. This was their land. These men were scattered in front of us like mud bricks with readied guns and pointed demands. In short order we retreated, as we had a hundred times before. There was no ambiguity in our orders and there was little fear of violence. We were simply to comply when our hosts wanted us to leave.

My comrade-in-arms, Matt, joined me as we left our tank and climbed into a nearby military jet. Matt would be the pilot. I sat to his left in the open-faced cockpit. Glancing out at the wings I noticed their unusually thin shape seemed too flat to be lift-producing. They also seemed rather crudely welded together. No matter, we would fly.

RIGHT WING

We decided to follow the railroad line en route to my hometown in North Dakota. The trip would surely be a short one from our current location (west-central Minnesota). However, once in the air, I became concerned that Matt was flying too low. We were frequently flying *under* the power lines which ran along railroad and, although I did not think we would hit the tracks below us, I feared we would hit a line or a pole. We had already come very close. I asked Matt if we could fly higher because of this and he said, "No, it's okay." The next pole we approached was coming too close. With my left hand on the seat beside me I felt a "ping!" "Matt!" I said, "We hit that one!" I was sure that we had clipped the support cable angling down from the pole we had just passed. Mike was unconcerned. He gazed calmly forward into the red-orange evening sky. "Matt, why can't we just fly a little higher? We're gonna get killed!" Matt finally admitted his problem. He was afraid of heights.

That said, Matt agreed to fly higher. He was a loyal comrade. We flew so high that I could see we were in a great cavernous room. The railroad was like a toy train track in a child's bedroom. There were other toy-like objects below and a desk that loomed like the White Cliffs of Dover. We could see four walls and a ceiling with massive electrical cables attached to it. The cables looped so low that our heads, sticking out of the open cockpit, began to bump them. We needed to go lower. In any case, our only exit was a small arched opening at the base of the far wall. We exited post-haste.

Shortly thereafter we approached my hometown from the east, still following the railway, which paralleled the county highway. As we passed the high school the road bent northward out of town and we saw a figure there, frantically waving his arms in the air. I recognized the man as my high school principal, so we flew over to him and landed softly just beyond his location. There were empty box cars near him and one was on fire. After a short conference we decided our services were not needed. So, after crudely fitting a piece of Plexiglas to the front of our carriage-like cockpit, we flew on.

We landed again about a mile north as we continued to follow the highway. There we talked to some people I knew and pointed out the scene of the fire.

dreamed in late February or early March, 1993, written 3/9/93

ANTHONY D. SINNER

Other Dimensions

Mary, my wife, and I were looking for a place to eat at a large shopping mall one evening. We stopped at a row of several eateries to see what was available. My cousin, Lynn, worked in one of the food places. We witnessed her speaking feverishly in French to another employee. She did not speak to us. I did not know that she spoke French.

Other things began to strike me as odd. There were people looking over their shoulders as they shopped, apparently trying to avoid being noticed. And, although I didn't normally wear glasses, I was wearing a pair with unusual thin rims.

The mall was dark and there was a long curved brick hallway leading from the food court. Mary and I followed this to a more brightly-lit area, entering through a normal-sized doorway. It was a large, square, cafeteria-like room with light blue walls. Inside there were a few men standing talking. The center of attention there was comedian Robin Williams, who was complaining about some financial problem. I interjected with sarcasm in my voice, "Why don't you just use the money from your last film?"

Robin erupted with a very genuine laughter that went on and on as he began to physically poke at me. Shortly, we were wrestling. I eventually flipped him over in an awkward way which left me unsure of how it actually happened. We made a truce and sat down at a cafeteria table. I took out my wallet and looked inside it. The bills there included two twenties, two ones, and two sevens. To make a further joke I gave Mr. Williams the two sevens. It was understood by everyone that seven dollar bills were no good in this dimension. At this time the idea that there were subtle differences between this world and the one I was used to began to gain more clarity.

Mary and I and a friend went out of the light-blue cafeteria to an adjacent room with exterior windows showing a daytime sky. The lights in this room were not on and it looked like this space hadn't been used in some time. Lining the walls were tables of electronic equipment and what looked like freestanding arcade video games. I went up to these game cabinets and examined them, one by one. As I moved along I could see my reflection in each of the darkened video monitors. But then I came upon an unfamiliar face. I immediately knew it was my reflection because the machine was off and the movements of the head and the blinking of the eyes corresponded to mine. But the face was reptilian with wide-set eyes and bright red, scale-faceted skin. I went to another screen. It showed the normal me. Next one. Nothing unusual. Then back to the screen with the strange reflection. Still there. I marveled at how broadly spaced my eyes were and how masculine my jaw and head looked. I decided that this screen must show what I look like in yet another dimension.

I called to the others to look at this screen as I hurried across the room to them. As I approached my friend I gestured to Mary and told her where to look. I saw her get up close to peer into the unusual screen. Almost immediately she was sucked headfirst through the screen, the soles of her shoes the last of her to be seen as she disappeared into the reptile dimension.

dreamed February or March, 1993, written 3/10/93

ANTHONY D. SINNER

Superman

I was Superman. I dressed in civilian clothes when not performing official duties – black turtleneck and gray slacks today – and I looked like actor Christopher Reeve. To some degree I knew the plot of the story I was living and so, acted accordingly.

There were two German agents, blonde, blue-eyed, and young – one male, one female. They lived in the boarding house where I lived. The female roomed across the hall, the male down the hall on the right. Mary (my real-life wife) lived down the hall on the left. The two agents spoke in thick accents and were known to be conspiring against me: Clark Kent, Superman, Christopher Reeve.

One day I met the female agent in the hallway and as we talked she took a few steps forward, backing me into my room. She was quite attractive. As we conversed about trivialities she laughed and smiled widely. Her teeth were kind of funny and crooked, but on her the effect was very charming.

I knew that the two were surveilling me, but I did not know their plans. So, one day I hid around the corner of the ivy-covered brick boarding house directly below my second story window and very near the front door. Making sure not to be unobserved, I watched the woman as she approached the door. She was wearing a grey turtleneck sweater and a khaki skirt and tall boots. When she was almost to the door I turned to fly up to my bedroom window so I would be in my room when she arrived at hers, suspecting nothing. I pointed my arms up over my head and jumped. Nothing. I jumped again and again, but I could not fly. I was a little embarrassed and thought to myself, "Isn't this the place in the story where I'm supposed to fly up to my window?"

That night I was feigning sleep with my door open so I could watch the goings-on across the hall. In the dim blue light of the night I could see the female agent in her bed from where I lay in mine. I wondered if she could see my eyes squinting open.

A night of suspicious goings-on ended with the two of us in a freestanding claw foot bath tub together, the German spy woman and I. Her skin was a pale, almost glowing, blue and mine was a warm tan. I was now body-builder Arnold Schwartzenegger instead of Christopher Reeve, but I was still Superman. The woman and I faced each other in the tub of clear water. I was on her right. Her chest was cleverly concealed by a tight suit of fake skin and so was her hip region. My genitals were concealed by a skin-colored pair of rubber shorts.

Although the woman was very attractive, I was only in the tub with her for reasons of spy-busting. It was, of course, my duty as Superman to defeat their plan using any methods available to me. Mary would certainly understand.

dreamed late February or early March, 1993, written 3/11/93

ANTHONY D. SINNER

Alien Invasion: College

While attending St. Luke's University I found myself having to drive to my hometown to return a car. The car was a 1970s vintage Dodge, light metallic olive-yellow with a red-brown vinyl top. I finished some homework, ran some errands in my dorm and began to make my way to the car. The commons was bustling on this warm, sunny day and several people called my name as I passed. I turned, gave a collective wave and hurried on.

On the way to my car I noticed another car. This car was much older – maybe from the 1950s – and was not at all shiny. It was patchy grey-white with a faded black top. The wheels were rusty and the tires were cracked. I realized that this car was also mine. I pulled on the door handle and, to my surprise, it opened. I thought to myself that I shouldn't have left it unlocked.

I began to drive away but had to backtrack to tie up another loose end and so ended up driving up into a construction zone on a very marginal road. Once inside the fenced area I saw the shape of a woman tugging at her under-wear. I say "the shape of a woman" because I could only see her and her surroundings in a glowing, mono-chromatic, night-vision way, like the unusual "solarized"

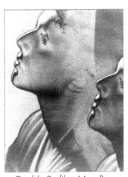

Double Profile - Man Ray

photographs created by Man Ray and Lee Miller in the 1920s.

She looked like she was made of smooth mud.

To respect her privacy, I turned the car around and prepared to leave. When I looked back I could see her normally again. She left through a gap in the fence, her red dress still hiked-up, exposing her black underwear.

I started to drive away but stopped as I heard some commotion behind me. From what I could make out it seemed someone had found a body. I got out and approached the small group of students at the site. As I got closer I glimpsed bones, white and shiny, almost like plastic. I spotted a human skull. Then two. Then a third. But I noticed one skull was not human. In fact, none of them were human. "Look at the eyes," I said. The eyes in the skulls were not holes but geometric bulges, like little geodesic domes.

Suddenly our attention was pulled skyward at the sound of aircraft. A large formation of military helicopters moved ominously across a suddenly war-torn sky. The sky appeared nearly overcast with the dense smoke and haze of an air battle. As we watched the formation of helicopters pass directly overhead it dissolved to expose a huge alien spacecraft.

Once again I was seeing in solarized-vision as snippets of battle scenes rushed across my view. I could hear TV news announcers recounting tales of horrible warfare and crises so dire it led me to believe the world itself was at stake. Soon I saw a close-up of an alien craft leaving Earth's atmosphere. A hatch opened and two english-speaking humans in space suits calmly jumped out, falling toward earth, leaving the derelict ship to drift in space. From a faraway view I could see, beyond the contrails of the ship and the two men, the long, cylindrical, crudely painted Earth.

dreamed and written 3/17/93

ANTHONY D. SINNER

Fishing at the Reservoir

On this day, a group of us were gathered around the northeast corner of my hometown's reservoir. Some of our number were readying a boat at the dock. I was part of a group on the banks of the dowdy little pond. Mary, my wife, was there and so were other family members and friends.

Already prepared to fish, I threw my line far out, watching the shiny lure plunk through the liquid surface. "Wham!" I got a big strike. I quickly reeled in and dragged a nice fish up onto shore. I was surprised to be able to land it so easily without a net. It was large, maybe ten pounds, a beautiful silvery fish, sleek and glistening with a small angular tail like a tuna and large iridescent scales. Everyone was impressed enough to show they were impressed, which is actually notable considering they were fishermen.

I threw my line out gain. And again a big fish. Like clockwork, two casts, two fish, the second as big and beautiful as the first. Not everyone was paying attention now, though. They were preparing for fishing themselves. Even I had the sense that I was just playing, casting off the shore for fun until the real fishing started out on the water.

I casted again. "Boom!" Same result. Three times in a row a big strike. I brought the fish in confidently and dragged it up the bank and onto the grass. The fish looked dead. It had just bitten my line a few seconds earlier and now it looked as if it had been rotting at the bottom for a week. It was almost as big as the first two fish, but it was not silver and shiny like the others.

Most of its scales were gone. I could see that the side of the fish was fleshy, white and rough. It was patchy, as if partially eaten or rotten, and it was covered with flies. I had noticed that the flies were on the fish when I pulled it from the water. I watched it closely and observed that it was alive and noticeably twitching. It was a disgusting sight and I felt a little embarrassed for having caught it. I didn't touch it, leaving it on the grass where it came to rest. I tried to hide my shock and embarrassment with a silly smile.

I threw my line out again. Immediately a bite, four in a row now. I was beginning to feel quite special, like a real fisherman, like it wasn't just luck. I pulled on the line hard, drawing my prey to the surface. A black and white, furry mass emerged a few yards in front of me. It was a skunk. And it was not hooked, rather it grasped my live minnow tightly in its front paws. I jerked the line hard but the skunk held on. It actually began to swim straight at us, straight for shore.

At this everyone scattered. I bolted, forsaking rod, reel, tackle, everything. We circled around the east end of the reservoir and, fortunately, the skunk did not follow, but rather stayed to feast on the fresh fish I had caught.

I led the exiled group of four or five to an area at the southeast corner of the pond where I knew of a concrete structure built on the sloping bank. The structure was like three sides of a box, open on the top and bottom and set into the bank so that there was a narrow gap near where the sloping shore met the water.

"Follow me!" I yelled, as I dived headfirst down the

ANTHONY D. SINNER

sloping embankment and into the box. But, as my head emerged from the narrow gap at the bottom of the box, I saw that the water was too close. With half my torso through the gap my face was almost in the water. I strained and arched my back to keep my head from going into the reservoir proper. Before I could back out, the others came down in rapid succession. Mary had followed first and her face had emerged through the narrow space. I tried to tell them to stop, to go back. But everyone was laughing and screaming, thrilled at the pile-up, not seeing our predicament. Thump, thump, thump! With each body coming down the slope, I was nudged farther and farther down. They had wedged me down so tight that I couldn't move my legs to squirm loose. I yelled for them to get off as my arms sank into the muddy shore, quickly failing to hold me out of the water.

dreamed summer 1993

Paralysis

Mary had left for work. It was early morning. The pale sky was gleaming through the gapping blinds, making me squint as I woke up. It was a normal morning.

Suddenly, outside my open bedroom door, I heard a voice. It was that of a young girl, maybe 6 or 7 years old. I did not recognize her voice. Startled at the idea of a stranger in the house, I pulled the covers up over my unclothed body. The girl spoke again, right outside my door. She was talking to someone, but it wasn't me. There was someone else in the house. Was she talking about me as she peered though my door? I strained to look, to turn my head, to lift my body to see through the door.

I could barley move, but I managed to lift my head and roll to my hands. The effort needed to move was enormous and when I had finally managed to get up I found myself suddenly – magically – prone again. I was flat on my back, pale morning sky again blinding me, the voices still in the house.

Now I heard a male adult farther away, possibly in the kitchen. "That's okay," he said, "let him take the big load." They were taking things. I sensed now that it was a family of robbers, mother, father, boy, and girl.

I struggled to move. I managed to sit up, keeping my eyes on the bedroom door. But, then I was suddenly down again, right where I started from. I tried to get up again. This time I sat up and put my feet on the floor, almost far enough to stand up. Maybe I could grab a robe and confront the intruders…but in a flash I was on my back again, under the covers, paralyzed.

ANTHONY D. SINNER

In actuality, Mary had gone to work and after a time I was able to break though my half-asleep, half-awake state to full wakefulness. The voices were gone, the sky blurred my eyes through the blinds, and I could move.

dreamed fall 1993

Triplets

After an extended and forgettable series of events I found myself with a woman who was in the throes of labor. She was lying on a long, cafeteria-style table, feet at one end, head toward the middle. She was not particularly large of belly, as one would expect a full-term pregnant woman to be, but she was certainly in the process of giving birth. Of this there could be no mistake.

Her face was quiet and her hair abundant, fine and dark. From my vantage point, standing to her left, helping to comfort her, she was so beautiful I could feel myself falling in love with her. She looked at me with an omnipresence, understandably preoccupied with bringing forth new lives. There would be more than one.

The first baby arrived. The attending father put the baby on the long table just beyond the woman's head. He stood at her right side, away from the action. He held her hand. Another baby came. I helped capture it and take it to be with its minutes-older sibling. In this baby's face I could see a clear resemblance to one of the expectant fathers. I said, "This one really looks like Mark!" But no sooner had the sound of my voice echoed away than I realized that my statement was ambiguous at best. There were five fathers of these children and three of them were named Mark. I was not one of the fathers.

A third baby came. At this moment I began to daydream about watches and clocks. I came upon a wonderful

ANTHONY D. SINNER

idea for improving timepieces. Within each clock and watch there should be a device that would monitor its timekeeping accuracy. In the event that a timepiece became the slightest bit off-time, this device of my invention would make the appropriate change to get the timepiece back on track. I was very excited about this possibly profitable invention.

All three children were now lying on the table near their mother. Two or three fathers were there to do paternal things. Then, something caught my eye about the triplets. They weren't spinning at the same speed. "Wait, look more closely," I thought. "Okay, it's okay." What I had failed to notice was that one of the triplets – which were now three concentric, scalloped, gold, jeweled, spinning rings, one, two and three inches in diameter, rising to the center – were not all spinning in the same direction.

The small ring had the same number of scallops as the second ring, and that one the same as the third, so by careful observation I could gauge the rate of their spins. The small ring and the large ring were going in the same direction, so I could line up a scallop and follow it around, judging the relative speeds. Rings one and three were in sync. It just looked odd because the second ring was running counter to the other two, making the rotation of the triplets look chaotic. And although I could not accurately measure the pace of the second ring relative to the others, its speed seemed about right. The babies would be fine.

dreamed and written 12/31/93

The Key Cult

We entered the humble rural house in the dark of night. In the kitchen an older man and several young men sat and stood, the elder presiding over the conversation under a low, central light fixture. The mood was friendly but sober.

Passing through the kitchen I emerged into what could have been a living room. But there was no furniture, just light-colored carpet and white walls and windows along one wall, darkened by the night outside. Across from the windows were built-in, painted-white cabinets, two doors, and the "key place."

The doors led to bedrooms and a bathroom. A woman gave me a brief tour of the building. Others in my group followed along. After the short tour we reentered the living room through a stairway room. By this time I felt well befriended by our guide and put my arm across her diminutive shoulders. She swept it away quickly, without embarrassment and gave me a look of "we are not nearly well-enough acquainted."

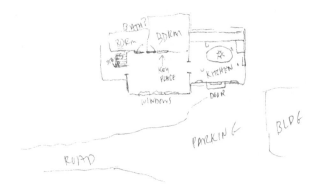

　　　　ANTHONY D. SINNER

I had met the woman earlier in the day while Mary and I ate lunch outdoors along a busy college-town street. She and her protégés were walking past us, apparently in some effort to be somewhere for a politically important purpose. A younger and more naive follower of hers stopped and expressed his hunger in a pleasant and goofy way and Mary was quick to offer him a large piece of chicken. With more time to think, I would have offered it because I wasn't at all hungry myself. He ate it quickly and left us the bones. The woman encouraged him to hurry.

She was a small woman, maybe 5 foot 2 and 95 pounds. She seemed street-smart and sure of herself. Even her tobacco-stained teeth could not diminish her charisma. She wore pants and a jean jacket, had dark brown hair, and intense brown eyes. She spoke with a little accent like she may have hailed from Missouri.

I stopped in front of the "key place" in the living room. The others were all somewhere else, talking and moving about. There was an area on the wall of cabinets where there were no cabinets. The area was about 3 feet wide and stretched from eye-level almost to the floor. At the top, extended about three inches forward and slanting slightly downward, was a clear plastic safety shield. The entirety of this area of the wall was covered with various conventional keyholes with keys in them. And on the floor, directly in front, was a pile of hundreds more keys. At the top, under the safety shield, was a row of brushed aluminum keyhole panels and a short section on the right that was shiny black. The keys in this upper section were smaller than the ones in the lower section.

I could run my hand over the whole area and feel the backs of dozens of keys tickle my palm. It was incredible, so many keys. Some of the keys would turn, some would not. But I didn't test many. Another plastic shield covered a special key and hole on the lower right. I saw that, unlike any of the others, this lock needed two keys inserted side-by-side to turn it. At this time, the two keys there were not even of the same type. These seemed like the most significant keyholes in the whole panel.

The woman returned to the living room and came over to me by the keys. She rattled off a long sentence or two that sounded a little like a fortune cookie and a little like a bible verse. She raised her eyes after finishing her lines and smiled knowingly. She was talking about *my* key. She was divining my personal future from my key, which was somehow plugged into the wall somewhere. We left the room in different directions.

I roamed the house for half an hour or so, stopping eventually in the kitchen to pass some time with the tough-but-friendly boys still gathered there. Then it was back to the keys.

My key was someplace on that wall. I realized that, in fact, I was missing *two* keys. I began to rummage through the pile and quickly found my *big* key. Now to find my other, smaller, one. There was a little cardboard box with key look-alikes, but no real keys. "Where the hell was my other key?" Several times I thought I'd found it. I did find a book with a tan cover about five by ten inches with a round, brown emblem on it. In it were numerous passages, short three-sentence verses. I paged all the way through and discovered, on the very last pages and on to the inside back cover, the exact words the woman had recited to me earlier. I kept looking for my *small* key. I could leave right away if I could only find it. I was getting anxious to leave.

I continued to dig through the keys on the floor. At the bottom of the pile, smashed down in a flattened twelve-pack cardboard was a soft lump. I opened it up and found…my *wash cloth*. It was damp and seemed to have something inside it. I carefully pulled the rust-colored cloth out while leaving the undisclosed amorphous object within it in the cardboard and out of sight. I thought it might be feces. I did not want to hold my wash cloth now.

At this time I began to suspect that the young gentleman who ate our chicken earlier in the day had taken several items from us during our brief encounter.

The woman returned. She sat down on her knees in

ANTHONY D. SINNER

front of me, realizing what I had been up to. I confronted her about her protégé who I suspected of taking our things. I didn't believe that *she* was behind his key-stealing, but I wanted to scold her for the behavior of her acolyte. She apologized and explained that it was difficult to control a mentally-handicapped individual. "Handicapped?" I asked. She went on to explain that the mentally-handicapped don't scare her much unless they don't have a southern accent. One that she knew of from the north swallowed his own eyeball. "There was no telling how may days it spent in his intestinal tract," she explained.

dreamed 3/27/94

BOOK OF
VERSES

Alien Invasion: Hometown

I was passively enjoying the expansive blue sky of a summer day when catastrophe struck. As I gazed through the picture window of my boyhood home the terrible thing I had always feared would happen, happened. A large commercial airliner flying across my view suddenly faltered, stalled, and plummeted helplessly toward the earth.

I stared, waiting for the tell-tale plume to rise, as the plane came in contact with the ground miles away from me. But instead, the sleek, ultra-modern aircraft plunged deep into the ground causing a great ring-mound of earth to swell up around it. The uprising earth spread like a tidal wave, beyond reasonable physical expectations for the size and speed of the plane. At this point I began to suspect that something other-worldly was at work.

The ground wave heaved up automobiles, sending them, driverless, rolling outward from the crash like surfers. A mini-van and other vehicles rolled in our direction. Eventually the van and another vehicle came to rest in our garage, parking themselves perfectly as if piloted by invisible, smirking alien beings.

I went down into the basement of my home, which was open to the garage. Strange phenomena were taking place there in direct relationship, it seemed, to the crash and the phantom vehicles. While my father reclined on the sofa, salt crystals had begun to form on the mortar between the bricks of the fireplace. As more salt formed it began to fall, grain

　　　　　ANTHONY D. SINNER

by grain, onto the floor around the hearth. It had accumulated already to an inch deep or more, like rubble at the foot of a tiny mountain.

As I examined the area more closely I saw that the brass and glass carriage lamp fixtures on either side of the fireplace weren't right. I opened one to find it was full of cottage cheese and raisins. Suddenly, the raisins burst out like shots from a gun, two, three, four times, in the direction of my father. He appeared to be hit, mostly in the head, and lay, stunned, eyes open. I'm not sure if he was hurt.

dreamed 4/12/94, written 4/14/94

A Night of Fitful Sleep

It was a warm day early in the fall term at St. Luke's University. There was a sunny and pleasant emotion pervading the day. I was in a building crowded with people. A bright sun came in through a wall of windows behind me. I started up a stairway that led to the top of a very tall lobby. One flight up, turn. I passed someone who said my name. "Hi, Tony," she said. It felt great to be recognized. I said, "Hi", calmly smiled and hurried on. On the next course of stairs I noticed that the pattern on the white and black granite steps made it almost impossible to distinguish one step from the next. But I bounded along, almost defying gravity with the help of the railing. I thought I must seem extra-virile to the women who knew me there. I bounded even more athletically. Top of the flight, turn.

Many people were coming down the third flight, so many that I could not find an easy way up. To the left, to the right, and finally, up the center. Many of the people were very young – nine or ten years old. I saw two of my friend's children and patted them each on the head as they passed on my right. Soon, I was at the top.

Now in an upper lobby, I noticed a mushroom-shaped pillar in the middle. At its base was a heavy jacket laying open. Inside, stitched edge to edge and up into the sleeves was an exact facsimile of the *USA Today* newspaper from just a day or two before. All the color and print and headlines had been duplicated perfectly in stitchery.

*   *   *

ANTHONY D. SINNER

I was at my grandmother's house in the country. I went to an upstairs corner room to see the view. I wanted to do a painting of what I could see from up there, an interior scene incorporating the landscape seen out the window. First perspective, no good. I went to the next room. The view from the doorway of this room was so sublime it made me well up with the rapture of its extraordinary beauty. Even so, I had a more important objective to pursue at that moment. I needed to go farther into the room to see if there was an *even more* rapturous view. I approached the window to take in the scenery and something seemed odd. With each step toward the window the perspective changed in an unexpected way: the background forest got bigger as the trees right outside the window stayed the same. Not a good look.

Scanning the hillside I was able to see the large pavilion my grandfather was working on. Admiring the scenic quality of the mountain valley, I thought, "Why don't they turn this place into a resort hotel? They're missing a great opportunity here."

Soon I was in the nearby town up the valley from my grandparent's home. From the center of town you could see the whole valley. It was breathtaking. Nearby they were demolishing a little brick building that said, "Rice Flour, Wheat Flour, Etc." on the side. Chatting with the owner, who wore a plaid sports coat, I found out that he thought the political climate was right to demolish the building. It wouldn't be an affront to the farmers at this time.

Then I saw smoke in the distance. The forest was on fire. I saw a fire plane dropping clouds of flame retardant on the fringes of the blaze. Dark smoke poured from amidst venerable pines, browned from drought. Three sides of the town were threatened. My escape was down the valley.

But in that direction, still in the town, I saw a spout of orange flame and sparks erupt. I looked again. It was magma. Two separate spouts were shooting glowing-hot rock into the air in irregular spurts. Some of the magma fell near me, splatting and turning dark as it hit the cool, paved street.

I turned to move through town up the valley. There I saw something I had been warned about: ill-conceived weapons testing. Three Power Rangers in their spandex and helmets were holding a long hose and nozzle in a parking lot near the side of a tall brick building. I hastened across what would soon be their line of fire. I could hear them speak of being ready as they backed up against the building, holding the hose, braced for a blast.

They fired. A laser beam-like stream of liquid fire flashed out, inadvertently igniting a meter-reader's three-wheeler. I turned quickly back to get to the town center, crossing over pools and streams of a clear, noxious liquid that seemed to be leaking from their weapon. I thought everything could explode at any moment.

9/8/94

ANTHONY D. SINNER

The Evil Genius

I had a friend who was a celebrated man. He was about sixty years old, short and bald. He was the inventor of wonderful, whimsical things and he was a philanthropist. He was one of the beautiful people, a genius. The fact that he held me in high esteem made me overlook his grandiosity, his materialism, his effusiveness. Mary and I and our friend Ken were recruited by this man to try out one of his new inventions. I was expending much effort trying to get Mary and Ken to like him.

The invention was an amusement park-type ride. It consisted of a ramp that descended and twisted and turned – a sort-of dry water slide. A metal track inscribed with two shallow channels was to guide us down. The track was so beaten and worn it looked like it had been in use for a hundred years already. We were to travel in separate carts that resembled shallow, hammered metal bathtubs. The ride was outdoors.

I went first down the steep starting ramp, quickly realizing that, if I didn't somehow compensate, my cart would shortly be going too fast to hold the track. So, I put my feet out the sides of my tub and managed to slow to a safe speed. Realizing Mary might soon be catching up behind me, I turned my head to check on our situation. She was indeed coming fast.

I scrambled to pull my tub off the track and let her by. As she passed, I yelled, "Mary, put your feet out!" She got the idea and, to my surprise, found a lever on either side of her within her cart. When she pulled on them sparks went flying and she began to decrease her speed. I felt like kind of a dope for using my feet.

I got back in my cart.

Mary was slowing at the bottom of the initial ramp section as I closed in on her, just before the first turn. Suddenly, she was ejected from her tub and buffeted awkwardly against the track. I managed to grab her just before she would have met one of several rectangular holes in the middle of the track, large enough to easily devour cart and rider, alike. Within each hole, inches below the rectangular opening, was a pair of huge meshing grinders, like evil oil drilling equipment. Their furious spinning evoked horrifying images of the human tragedy barely avoided. Ken pulled up behind us, seeing what had happened. I began to grow angry that we had been put in such a dangerous situation.

As dust puffed from the menacing grinder holes we jumped off the ramp and continued in the direction our carts had been taking us, but now on foot. Ultimately, this led us into a very large warehouse-type building. Once inside we reached the end of the metal track and came upon a mountain of cardboard boxes, all packed full of some unknown commodity, stacked against a cinder block wall. We climbed to the top of the box pile and were joined by a robust red-haired woman who sat with us as we attempted to collect our wits after our recent shock.

Before long the genius approached, like a favorite uncle with treats. His pale face smiled a toothy smile. He talked to us from the bottom of the mountain of boxes. He sensed our anger and – always smiling – apologized about the mishap on the ramp ride. "We'll just have to work harder to get it right," he said.

I descended the mountain to confront him. Feeling that our relationship was the only string I could pull, I said, "If I was to die tomorrow, you and I would never again be friends!" I tried to mean that as of that moment I did not consider him a friend of mine and my feelings would not change overnight. I knew he took my point, but he was all smiles, showing no real remorse. He seemed to care only about his next invention, his next conquest, his empire.

I went back to the top of the stacked boxes. The genius

ANTHONY D. SINNER

walked across the room to an area where his burly assistant-cum-bodyguard was readying another perilous game. There were two card tables, each with a hole in the middle. The good-looking, well-groomed assistant was dumping a load of sand from a skid-loader. A sense of foreboding came over me as I watched the scene play out. I was the only one of us who knew the genius well enough to predict his behavior, except maybe for the red-haired amazon who seemed to have a history with him.

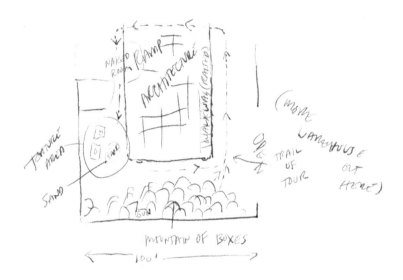

The genius motioned up to us. He wanted Mary and Ken. Innocently, they complied, trudging down the mountain like calves to slaughter. A fury of helplessness was building inside me. I wanted to kill the genius. And we had a gun.

By now we all knew there was a loaded pistol at the top of the pile of boxes. The genius knew it, too. He seemed to be tempting us to try and use it. While monitoring the assembly of the apparatus his assistant was preparing for Mary and Ken, he would glance up at the red-haired woman and I as if to ask, "Aren't you going to try it?"

I wanted the woman to get the gun. "You know how to shoot, don't you?" I asked. "You could do it better than me, I'm sure." Neither of us could bring ourself to do it. We were completely helpless against the evil genius. I was beside myself. I was beaten that easily.

As if to flaunt his great power over us the genius next took the red-haired woman and I on a guided tour of the facility, apparently expecting nothing but fawning adoration and rapt attention. While on the tour I noticed that my female companion was very quiet ... and beautiful. After showing us a few uninteresting areas, the genius led us to a room with a scene of love-making on the wall. At this time the woman and I were unclothed. She was even more beautiful without her jeans and plaid shirt.

But before I could be much more enamored with her we emerged at the site of the sand torture. We had come full-circle on our tour.

Now I was face to face with my despair again. I saw Mary before me. She sat in a pile of sand that was slowly engulfing her, poured on relentlessly by the genius' assistant. Her head was stuck through the hole in one of the tabletops and her mouth was stuffed with a an object shaped like a bar of soap but made of sand.

I reached over to help her but I didn't know what to do. The assistant came up beside me and I stood up quickly and planted my elbow on his jaw. Dumbfounded, he tried to push me. I reached down and lifted Mary out of the sand trap and removed her gag. I held her and we cried.

The bully assistant looked as if he had finally realized

ANTHONY D. SINNER

that this was all too mean and stupid, and that he was through
doing the bidding of the evil genius.

We were safe.

10/3/94

Went Home Sick

I came home sick from work one day and went straight to bed. I had this dream.

I was at work and feeling ill. I felt I needed to go home, but just as I was about to leave I noticed a customer at the counter. I wanted to let my co-worker, Cindy, know about the customer without letting her know I was still there. I wanted to avoid getting involved in something that would delay my departure.

I would ring the shop counter bell to alert Cindy and then dash away before she came out. But, just as I got to the bell, Cindy came out and saw me. I would stay a little longer and finish a few things.

As I blundered though a job or two I felt sicker and sicker. Soon a revelation came to me and I tried to pass it on to my three cohorts in the shop. I said to them, "Y'know, I'm probably at home in bed right now and still I'm stuck here doing this!"

They didn't say much. I said it to everyone, each in turn. I related the idea several times. "I bet I'm at home in bed right now, sleeping, and still I can't leave this place!" Cindy paused from what she was doing and looked at me like I was losing my mind. Nobody was taking me very seriously.

I felt even more ill as I worked on another project. I finally decided, "To hell with it," and slumped over on the table, asleep.

dreamed 10/12/94 afternoon, written 10/13/94 evening

ANTHONY D. SINNER

Dustin Hoffman

The actor Dustin Hoffman came to the frame shop. Two of his brothers had been in earlier, but this was the real guy, the famous actor. And I was going to wait on him.

My philosophy, as always, was to treat an important person just like anyone else. I prided myself on my objectivity and composure in such situations.

The two of us went over to an alternate picture framing sales counter and I began to help him decide what would be right for his pieces. Dustin was wearing a plain pullover sweater and had long, bushy, 1970s hair. He looked young. I thought that this must be Dustin in his early thirties.

He wanted to frame several photograph-collage pieces that he, himself, had made. All of the pieces consisted of an arctic scene with open water in the foreground. In the backgrounds were glaciers, mountains or icebergs. Pasted to each of these scenes was one or two nude, swimming figures, placed to suggest they were in the water. The heads of the figures were replaced with the heads of primitive statuary or some other incongruous representation of a head, sometimes that of an animal. The base picture was in color – white mountains and ice blue water. The swimming figures were in black and white and the heads were pink to orange.

I was just beginning to get down to business with Mr. Hoffman when my mother came in and, sneaking up behind Dustin, poked her index fingers into his ribs. "Hi there!" she exclaimed. I stared in horror as she walked around to my side of the counter to face Dustin. She was smiling giddily, glancing back and forth between me and Dustin. I thought, "Mom, what are you doing? Don't you see how composed I've been?" After a bit more mugging, Dustin and Mom began to exchange pleasantries and I realized that they were actually old friends. "Since when?" I thought.

Later, Mom and I exited out the back door of the store. A couple of semi-trailer trucks were maneuvering in the cramped parking lot. One truck turned sharply in front of us and curled up a swath of asphalt as wide as the truck, like a big, black lasagna noodle.

Mom moved deftly through the traffic as I started and stopped, balking just outside the door. Without a flinch, she headed for Dad and the waiting car. Meanwhile, I jumped around the corner of the building to avoid another wave of heavy vehicles. In front of me was a tall, white crane swinging violently back and forth. I was trapped between swiftly moving trucks on all sides and a crane about to fall on me.

dreamed 10/28/94

Will's Foot and Arm

I was at my childhood home in rural North Dakota, visiting Mom and Dad. Several of my brothers and sisters were there. I found myself urinating in the basement shower in the presence of Mary, my wife. My urine was thick and brown and fell in stalagmite-like piles on the shower floor. I opined that perhaps I had hepatitis. Mary was not noticeably concerned. I turned on the shower to wash away the urine piles, but the stuff was so substantial it took considerable time and effort to do it.

I went upstairs where I found people eating at the dining room table. My sister and brother-in-law had brought two kinds of bread-maker breads for everyone to enjoy. I was in good humor and feeling really healthy, despite my presumed hepatitis.

When Dad came to the table I decided to ask him, the old hepatitis warrior, what he thought of my symptoms. He became increasingly attentive as I ended with the anecdote about the difficult-to-wash-down piles. He was interested, but not as upset as I would have expected him to be, knowing my father.

I went back downstairs. I contemplated my foot, specifically my heel. It was very narrow. I thought about my friend Will's foot and heel. I put our two right feet in front of me, heels pointing in my direction. Will's heel was very broad. I associated this with Will's character and his physical nature. I wondered, "Was this very broad, skipping-stone heel intrinsically connected to Will's natural ability to leap and lope? Was it tied to his ability to work hard?"

I attached his foot to my leg, at the ankle. I walked. It

felt strange. It felt almost like what I imagined an amputation to be like in its ability to evoke shock and grief. I put on Will's right arm. It was longer than my left arm when I extended them together. Like the foot, it was shaped differently than my body. The hair was in a different pattern, the skin was softer, the angles foreign. I had a pit in my stomach.

I held the arm up again. I had put his left arm on my right side. It felt very awkward and didn't function comfortably.

Panic built inside me, thinking of my unattached body parts, waiting for reattachment. Where are they? Can they even be put back on? A thick claustrophobic feeling fell on me as I began to fear that I lacked the dexterity, with Will's clumsy arm, to reattach my own limbs.

3/2/95

Downtown

I lived downtown. I could walk around the tall buildings and find my way intuitively back to where I lived. I passed by my boss on the street. He was very solemn and straight-faced, leading a group of businessmen on a tour of some kind. He noticed me peripherally but did not publicly acknowledge me. He and his entourage looked so serious I was tempted, more than once as our paths crossed, to blurt out something like, "What's this, Dave, a parade of the league of fascist entrepreneurs?" I actually opened my mouth to spew this sarcasm at one point, but thought better of it and walked on.

I was on a familiar block now, just a short distance from the coffee shop and café on the storefront level of my building. I was walking fairly briskly on a sidewalk full of people. Behind me strode two women, one pushing a stroller with a baby in it. She drove it directly into the back of my ankles. I jumped forward to put a safe distance between myself and the stroller. But soon she was on me again, not just bumping, but keeping constant contact with me. She had to know she was doing it, I thought. Finally I turned, reaching over the baby below me, and grabbed the tubular steel handle. Inexplicably, she kept pushing. I tried to wrest the stroller from her grasp. She held tight. I pushed and pulled and began to tip the stroller sideways. I could have torn it away from her and thrown the stroller right down on the sidewalk, but I noticed the baby. It was almost falling out. I let go and ran ahead.

Soon I had reached the entrance to the café. It was

a friendly, familiar place, a daily contact for me since it was connected to the lobby of the building I lived in. I went down a short hallway and to the west door. At the entrance were two men, seated, talking. One was beside the door and one was on a stool in the doorway. The person ahead of me squeezed through and I thought, "Surely, I can also fit through, being so slim. He could be no slimmer that me." I walked right into the gap and couldn't make it. I was stuck between the guy seated there and the door frame. Peeved, the man got up, moved his stool into the café, and let me through. He wasn't looking to be thanked. I scurried by.

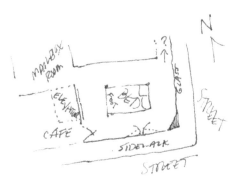

Straight through the café and out the east door, I entered the lobby of my building, which also happened to be my bedroom. Polished granite floors, two walls of glass from floor to ceiling, city sidewalks just outside. At the foot of my bed were elevator doors, now open to the guts of the shaft inside – out of order. Next to the elevator was a door that led to a softly lit room where people pulled mail from their boxes.

Today maybe no one would have to come through my bedroom. Previously, they may have wanted to come from the café, or from the mail room, or from the streets through the big glass doors to get to the elevator. But they couldn't use the elevator just now. What a beautiful day!

ANTHONY D. SINNER

I sat on my bed and contemplated why my apartment wasn't upstairs on the twenty-whateverth floor like usual, next to the people I knew. I pulled things out of my pockets – wallet, keys – and sat, slumped, releasing the sighs of another day. I noticed an unidentified ring of keys lying on the bed. On the ring was a worn, plastic, hotel-type tag that was light blue, the same color as my bedspread. From the inscriptions on the tag I began to realize that these were keys to the resort my wife's family would stay at the following summer.

Just then a policeman appeared next to my bed, having come in from the café. "What are these?" he asked, accusatorily, as he picked up the keys. I made half a grab for them, stopping the impulse in time. I stammered a moment, thinking on one hand that these weren't my keys and I could get in trouble, and on the other hand that I was the guardian of these keys since my wife's family would certainly need them.

The policeman, who happened to look exactly like the singer and actor Hoyt Axton, moved toward the glass doors that opened to the street. I jumped up and confronted him at the there. He wore a name tag indicating his name was Clan, Clan Olsen. I thought it was a dumb name and I wanted to say so, but I held my tongue. "Those are my keys," I said.

Clan was evasive. His glance flirted with passersby, as if he was looking for lawbreakers. "How do I know these are yours?" He was expressionless except for a hint of self-satisfaction.

I said, "Look, don't you think I know people in this building?" He remained unimpressed.

dreamed January, 1995, written 3/2/95

Affair at the White House

I was at the White House preparing for an affair of some kind. Two other important gentlemen and I were getting dressed for the event in a nicely appointed room. We were discussing and comparing our choices of dress – very formal, of course, but not without individuality. Shiny, satiny, monochrome, and paisley vests were in question at the moment.

I had something to give to President Reagan before he went out to present himself. He was in his room and almost ready. It was very critical that the President have this item I held. Even though he seemed rather oblivious to this thing, there were those making sure he had it. The item was a clear plastic fast-food packet of Italian dressing which was slightly greasy on the outside. I didn't know if it was leaking or alternatively, had come into contact with another leaky packet. I gave it to the President and he gingerly put it in his jacket pocket. A stain would be inevitable.

Later we were wandering around the grounds looking for the right door to enter. There were some kids with real or replica guns and some secret service people around. Someone pointed to a door. We entered. It opened to a stairway leading downward. It would descend eight or ten steps, then a landing, turn a corner 180 degrees, and go down again eight or ten steps, etc., counterclockwise.

There was a solid tiled wall running up the center of the stairwell, so you couldn't look over the edge to see how far down it went. I began to walk down, one, two, three flights, and

ANTHONY D. SINNER

then decided to make it faster and easier. I grabbed a large shovel and sat down in the pan of the shovel with the handle sticking up between my legs. I grabbed the handle with both hands and proceeded downward, sliding like on a sled. I was able to turn the corners by steering with the handle and away I went, flight after flight of sheer ecstasy. I never passed a door. I just kept going down, down, down. I was just waiting for the bottom to meet me.

written 4/21/95, dreamed a few years earlier

A Visit to the Buddhists

We were out at night, enjoying the air and the sights and sounds of downtown. The sky was dark. We skipped and played as we walked. Filled with ourselves, we joked and teased as the blocks passed unnoticed. We had been to our main destination earlier that evening and were now just finding our way to the car. Our small group included my wife, Mary, and our friend, Ken.

We came upon a wooden, light-colored, flat-faced building that crowded the sidewalk. The lights were on. Instead of passing it by like the hundred other buildings on our journey that night, we went in. Inside, there was a clear, quiet feeling. People were dressed in cloth wraps. The large square window openings were covered only with insect screens. In a few moments, we were in conversation with the people there. I ended up being the focus of conversation on our side.

After a time I realized that everyone in the house was female, from young girls in their early teens to elderly women. I found out through conversation that this was a place for Buddhists, a monastery for women.

An authoritative, middle-aged woman serenely offered me a cinnamon roll. She said I must give her something in return, "a sandwich." I accepted the food not knowing exactly how I would repay her.

I sat with them for a while, long enough for Ken, Mary and the others to disappear. I could hear them making their way back to the street. But I continued to converse, enthralled and delighted with the interaction in this unusual place.

ANTHONY D. SINNER

A young Buddhist, maybe 18 years old or so, who had the look of someone from Southeast Asia or the Pacific islands, took a special interest in me. In fact, as the minutes passed, I became quite infatuated with the attractive, poised novice.

I grew interested in asking her a specific question. I didn't know exactly how her superiors would take the query, so I was trying to time it right. Three or four times the chance would arise and dissipate. I wanted to ask her, "Why did you join the Buddhists?"

I showed the young Buddhist a book I had. We paged through it as I told her about it. Soon I began to peel back the surface of a page to reveal what was inside. Underneath the tissue layer was a thin sheet of chocolate, etched with the same words as the paper that had covered it. I went on to remove the tissue on the back side of the chocolate page and then ate some of the page. I gave some to the novice.

Several unwrappings ensued, each of us devouring entire pages. I felt that this could be my repayment for the earlier gift of food.

I never did ask my question.

dreamed 8/25/95

My Mother had a Baby

My mother had another baby. It had a cute little face which seemed to show a hint of progeria, and looked, upon careful examination, just like my mother's. It had a broad, downward-sloping nose that hung over its lovable grin. It gazed at our mother and when she smiled at it her expression and features looked just the same as the newborn's. I also noticed a distinctive extra flap on the rim of the right nostril that was evident in both of them.

The child was slightly mobile and we wanted to teach it to walk. It had long skinny legs with two toes at the end of each. It had no neck to speak of and two skinny arms sprouted from its plump body. The child resembled a cross between a frog and a grasshopper and was only about three inches tall.

With some coaxing, it began to walk and then began to hop precariously from one leg to the other, balancing momentarily between hops. At first its movements were herky-jerky, but after a short time it seemed to gain confidence and would pump its

ANTHONY D. SINNER

legs so fast they became a blur. When the furious dance paused it would be standing again on one leg, where it would sway for a moment or two and then dance again. It seemed somewhat aware that it possessed amazing abilities.

Its precociousness was further demonstrated when it converted itself into an investing machine. In this mode it was an 18- by 24-inch slab of marble with a glass dome and some workings underneath.

It opened its dome and out sprang a stack of bills. It instructed me how to invest these funds at a nearby automated teller machine. We were very impressed with the baby's talent.

dreamed early February, 1996

Khrushchev and Duchamp

Several young Americans and I were visiting the Soviet Union. We were treated to myriad demonstrations of how wonderful were the lives of the people who lived there. Lots of pomp and circumstance and regular folk doing extraordinary things, such as walking, fully dressed, in cold weather, into a lake. When a man and woman performed this ritual my impression was that it was intended to show the solidarity of the Soviet family.

Nikita S. Khrushchev invited us to visit him one day. He was a very nice man with an affable character that made us warm to him immediately. Late in the day, as our group walked out to a parade, he held my hand. He looked at me with a sparkly smile and remarked that, for a skinny man I sweat like someone much heavier. I was not sweating at the time, but I thought he must have noticed me perspiring earlier in the day. He said he liked me because I was so unusual.

Later we were in a dark room with a darkened television in the corner. Behind the television was a man fixing it. We were shown, in a book, a work by artist Marcel Duchamp. It was one I had never seen before, but I could see it was maybe the precursor to a later, slightly different work. I approached the man behind the television as he worked. It was Mr. Duchamp, himself. I asked him if we had seen this precursor-piece earlier, when he had lectured to us about his art. I didn't think we had. He affirmed that we had not, but declined to explain further.

The Duchamp artwork we saw consisted of concentric

circular regions on a horizontal rectangular canvas. The center circle was salmony-red, the next was baby blue, and the outer, cut-off section was a darker sky-blue. In each section, several

elongated oval shapes were randomly scattered. Within each of these shapes was a representation of a pair of crushed eyeglasses with heavy dark rims and an eye peering out of one lens. The ovals were baby-blue in the darker sky-blue region, sky-blue in the baby blue region, and salmony-pink in the red, central region. The borders between regions and around the oval shapes were highlighted by clean white lines.

dreamed March 13th or 14th, 1996

The Swelling Sea

I was near a great body of water, a sea. The water was bounded by a right angle of land. I could see a sheltering coast far away. There was a narrow ochre-yellow, strip of sandy clay which formed a flimsy boundary between the water and a long, L-shaped building, which paralleled it. The width of this beach varied from ten to twenty feet.

I watched the water heave and build to great heights just a short distance out in the bay. It would swell repeatedly and violently under the dusky-green, overcast sky. I watched from inside the L-shaped building as I walked down the long, window-lined hallway heading to the bend of the L. The sea swelled again and again, building fiercely toward this spot where the shoreline went in perpendicular directions, south and west, forcing the stirring liquid to a point.

I anticipated that the water would crash down and spread out on the narrow strip of beach, lapping at the building, or worse. But there were no breakers, no froth. The heaving sea would build like a beast but recede without pouncing. I went out on the water. I rode the wave for a few moments, without board or boat, feeling ecstatic and unafraid. I could have ridden far out and not returned, but I returned to that vulnerable spot.

Back inside the building, at the place where the west wing met the south wing, I noticed a desk like one you would see at an auto repair shop and a uniformed, inattentive man behind it. There was no other furniture in the room and nothing on the walls. Next to the desk two large side-by-side garage doors were

ANTHONY D. SINNER

open to a larger garage or warehouse area. A man in street clothes stood there with a camera around his neck.

The walls were stucco and went up 15 feet or so to the ceiling of a 30 foot square room. Where wall met ceiling the dirty, peach-colored stucco curved with a radius of three feet, joined smoothly like adobe.

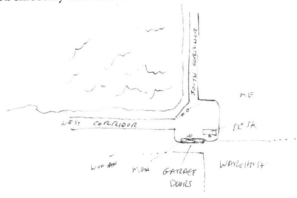

I went to look out the window. The sea was still swelling and receding, never breaking, like an ocean breathing. Others watched it, too. I turned toward the back of the room, when suddenly, "Shwoom!" The wave I had always expected to break upon us finally did and came crashing through the wall of windows. I knew what had happened, still feeling the rhythm of the sea, even with my back to it as it hit.

My world was white foam. I felt the tepid whorl surge in, carrying me up over the place where the man behind the desk had been. I sensed the torrent pass beneath me and through the garage doors as it filled the room and held me against the curved cove of the stucco ceiling.

I still could not see. Everything was churning white. I was surprised to be breathing easily in the water and not afraid.

dreamed the second week of September, 1996

Children Hiding in the Car

Mary and I were returning from a grocery run in our Honda Civic Wagon when I was startled by the sound of giggling coming from the rear of the car. I whirled around from the passenger's seat and could see a little girl, poking her head out the side of the car through a small door behind the left rear tire. She was laughing and playing and I could hear the voice of another child, too.

I had forgotten that two children, a boy and a girl, had been stowing away under the floor in the hatch section of our car for almost two and a half years. Mary had not forgotten and was not startled in any way.

Immediately a cacophony of anxious thoughts filled my head. "Where were their parents? Are we in trouble for not returning them to their family? How have they survived? What do they eat? When do they bathe? Do they go out at night? How do they survive the cruel Midwest winters in a parked car in the driveway of my home?"

I was feeling really panicky about it all when the two emerged from under the floor and sat contentedly in the back seat, the boy behind me, the girl behind Mary. Impulsively, I reached out and touched the boy's arm. It felt grimy, as if he had not washed in weeks or months. He jumped back just far enough

ANTHONY D. SINNER

to break contact and he and his sister continued with their happy play.

They were about the same age, but the girl was definitely the boss. I got the feeling that it was her initiative that brought the two here, possibly from an abusive family situation. No doubt they were hiding. But they were still loving it after all this time. They seemed to have developed their own little world under the floor of the car where their fantasies could fuel endless fun.

They didn't look familiar to me. The girl had shoulder-length, light brown hair and a face, broad with a perpetual smile of mischief. The boy's hair was almost bowl-cut, same color, and his face was more oval and not as smiley. He followed his sister's lead. He wore a light blue velour shirt and she wore a dark purple, knit turtleneck.

Mary was not very concerned and continued to drive. My panic had not faded much since exchanging greetings with the two. I thought of the trouble we could be in for harboring these children, albeit unwittingly. And the unknown circumstances and consequences of their sheer existence...what about that?

The children went back under the floor, where we still heard them playing from time to time. It startled me each time.

dreamed 12/14/96, about 4am

Long Day in a Strange Town Very Near the Ocean

It was a bright, sunny day and the world was bathed in a faded blue light. I was outdoors and very near the ocean, but I could not see the water from where I was. In an area in front of a strip mall I was riding bikes with some people I did not know. The bikes were of an extraordinary new design and it was a singular joy just to ride one. They were medium-sized bikes and were capable of the most wondrous feats. I watched the other riders, who seemed to have a practiced knowledge of how to use the bike, and imitated them while following them around. The bikes were lithe and speedy and had an affinity for balancing. The only feature that made them obviously different from, say, the average mountain bike was that you could pedal frontwards or backwards. I couldn't tell how the others were braking, exactly, but everything we did seemed so intuitive, so natural. At any time while riding it was possible to go up on one wheel, the front or the back, and while on ice one could pirouette endlessly, sprawling out within inches of the ice like a skater in a death spin.

While we were riding up and down the block we went on sidewalks that abutted sandy areas (presumably close to the beach) and in and out of an open-air department store, down aisles of clearance merchandise and racks of clothes and handbags.

These bikes were not ours. We were test-riders – some of us apparently off the street – for this phenomenal new product. I felt insecure about my riding as the others seemed somehow to be in the bike-testing life, but I was competitive and determined to keep up. And I thought I pretty-much did.

When the biking was done I wandered through some glass doors to a large warehouse-store and then into the adjoining department store. I was now walking down the aisles wearing only some skimpy shorts and a T-shirt, knotted up in front to show a little tummy.

Some nice people ushered me over to a place where others were gathering for a meeting. They wanted me there even though we all knew I had no knowledge of this place, the organization or its people. Some people were sitting on the floor, and some, including me, in cheap designer plastic stacking chairs. It appeared that most people knew each other and they were fully dressed. I began to feel really naked and uncomfortable so I got up and left, moving to another part of the store toward the street and daylight.

I was approached there by two very stylishly dressed individuals, one male, one female, who began to ask me about doing some modeling. The woman explained to me (my shirt was now off) that I would be standing with one hand behind my back, and the female model would be standing next to me, one hand over her breast. I took this to mean she would have one breast exposed, being half-naked like me. This shoot was to happen immediately. There seemed to be a level of conspiracy in this, similar to the level of conspiracy in the survey-taking that takes place at malls. They appeared to have every right to go about this business. Common courtesy seemed to be our only bond.

Finally, with my approval amounting to my saying nothing, I was led by a man to the department store photo studio where there was a bed. He and I stood by the bed, him with his headset and clipboard, me with my shorts on and my shirt in my hand. Around us were half a dozen support people and plenty of artificial lighting.

In the small bed were two people who, he assured me, were sleeping. Indeed they appeared to be, albeit fitfully, as they occasionally rolled beneath the covers. The two were apparently identical twin brothers, tall and thin, clean shaven with fluffy, rooster-top haircuts. They seemed to be wearing nothing but the bedclothes. The man told me to sit on the bed where the covers were obviously concealing one of the twins. He asked me to sit on a spot that was clearly the head of the twin on my side of the bed.

For a while now I had been figuring that the plan for the shoot no longer involved a half-naked woman. I began to get very apprehensive. If I get into this, what sort of things are going to be happening? Was it some sort of porn thing? I told the man decisively that I would not sit on that person's head. And this was out of sympathy for the person about to be abused, rather than fear of some sexual pretext. The man assured me all would be fine, speaking in a very matter-of-fact, knowing way. Saying something like, "We do this all the time and we know what we're doing, but we also respect you and your concerns."

Soon, the fitful sleepers tossed and turned again, throwing all the covers off the twin nearest me and exposing his naked derriere, which was flat and dirty, as if he had been sitting on a cement floor for half a day.

I begged off and decided to leave, half expecting them to follow me and use any means permissible to get me to come back to the shoot. Ultimately, they did not. I imagined what they might be doing as I walked away, not looking back. But I will never know their reaction. I was shortly out in the open air and heading back to the glass doors that led to the warehouse-store. I was once again fully clothed.

In the store I began to have a sense of the pervasive theme of the whole place, very modern, very hip, very cutting-edge, and everyone happy, self-controlled and very comfortable in their role. It was creepy, but fascinating.

Next, I came across a sporting event, like a theatrically-staged basketball game. I looked though a mesh gate, like the ones that cover mall store entrances at night, and even though there was an official activity going on inside, the only light at all was coming from the common area behind me. Beyond the foreground figures I could see only an incalculable dark space.

The "players" were dressed in circa 1975 basketball uniforms, standing on nicely arranged individual platforms of various heights like statues would stand on. The platforms were dirty, gray crate-like boxes. A group of "players" stood on a set of these crates at each end of a ball court. Each group wore white uniforms with red trim and numbers. They played enthusiastically as a dirty gray object was passed between them. Behind each group's highest and rear-most player was a traditional, glass-backed basketball goal, but I did not see it come into play

I left and went back to the open-air area where a bike-tester told me he got up to 32 miles per hour on his bike. So I got on a bike and we rode off together in the direction of the ostensible ocean. I looked for a speedometer on my bike but did not find one. Our ride ended as we encountered a chain-link fence and could get no closer to the supposed sea.

Eventually, I went back to the warehouse area, noticing now that there were a lot of fences and barriers limiting my movements. I pushed on one of the store gates, behind which all was dark, and I found that I could easily swing it up and out of the way to get through. Once inside I was walking through aisles of faded-yellow, metal store shelves containing hardware and sporting goods. Suddenly, from above and behind, I heard a booming voice which said, "I am the Sun God, Ra, and I am here to smite you!" And down upon me he fell. Being three times my height, his head landed ten feet in front of me where it detached from his body like a doll's head. It was plaster and cloth and was formed into a crude elongated box. The rest of his blue-robed, doll body was even more crudely constructed.

As it turned out, Ra had a human-sized sidekick, made of regular sturdy flesh, who followed me as I continued on, unhurt by the Sun God's attack. This smart-alecky, parasitic personage was a crafty devil and shadowed me persistently despite my efforts to leave him behind.

I moved on until I noticed another dimly lit arena off in the dark. Again, there was a court of some kind, maybe the size of a hockey rink. On the court the handful of contestants, divided into two teams, were each driving a dune-buggy-sized official game vehicle. There were referees guiding play, which I couldn't make heads nor tails of. It was like this was one of the first games ever played of this kind, and everyone was very patient and happy just to be involved. The technology and design were certainly the latest. I left shortly, shadowed by the Sun God's little friend.

Next, I moved in the direction of the assumed ocean. By now my sinister shadow went nearly unnoticed. I (we) walked past the open-air department store area and eventually came to what seemed like an abandoned stock yard. This enclosed space was maybe one hundred feet square with a floor that looked like a mix of sand and manure. I could see through a chain-link fence across to a wooden fence on the opposite side, glints of sunlight leaking between ragged wooden boards. Beyond this fence was the imagined beach and ocean. A tin roof covered the yard about twenty feet above my head. As I pondered crossing the area we were joined by a young woman and a boy.

Suddenly, we heard a great slurping sound. Then off to our right, out of an arched opening in a concrete wall came a most revolting creature. Brown and wet and undulating, a gargantuan worm slithered out across the sandy floor. As its long body stretched farther and farther from its opening its leading end got progressively thinner. It searched blindly around the yard, its visible body now extended to a full seventy-five feet, its fore end as tiny as a normal earthworm, the other end never leaving the opening in the wall.

When the worm concluded its frightening ritual of extension and proceeded to retract itself back into its hole I decided it would be a good time to try to cross the stockyard. The way out seemed to be to the right, near the worm hole. We all jumped the chain-link fence and headed across. As we considered how to get out at the chosen spot, we heard the great slurping sound again.

I was near the archway as the creature began to emerge. Closer to it now I could see its reddish tint and a texture like foam rubber. It was four feet in diameter, fully occupying the opening through which it slithered. Horrified, we all ran back in the direction of the chain link fence. As I scampered I noticed that directly in front of the archway was a large metal wicket, slightly smaller than the archway and meant, I thought, to corral the back end of the worm and keep it from ever getting loose altogether. The worm undulated and pulsed and got very thin again. As it crossed my path I jumped over it, the end of it this time splitting into several tendrils, one of which went searching into another hole in the wall.

The woman, the boy and the shadow stayed clear of the creature on their way back to the fence. I carefully avoided one thin, blind tendril which I feared would grab my leg if it happened to brush against me. Then, as a group we scaled the fence with the sickening slurping sound still in our ears.

The shadow man and I then jumped another fence to enter an adjacent yard which held heavy equipment. This area, too, was impenetrable on the sea side, so I hopped on a fire truck and began to drive out in the other direction (my shadow appropriated a truck, too, and I did not see him again). As I drove away I was aware of how sluggish the acceleration was on a fire truck, but soon I got up to street speed. I saw official-looking people standing in the road ahead, in front of the department store and warehouse. Thinking they would stop me for stealing a fire truck, I turned right at my first chance and headed away from them.

Moments later I arrived at the town square and pulled over into the sandy parking lot there. I cut in front of a pick-up truck attempting to park just outside the lot and its occupants flagged me down. I did not recognize them, but came to believe they were old friends of mine. When I got out of the truck I saw it was listing badly to the driver's side in the soft sand so, with a mighty heave, I righted it.

I began to sense that any of the side streets leading from the town square would terminate in an impassable fence, so I went with my friends into a turn-of-the-century office building. The old wood floors creaked proudly as we walked into a side room where a man was resting in an antique office chair. I looked out his window and saw a railroad yard with layers and layers of fences. Near one of the fences was a small group of crows, each one about ten feet tall.

2/6/02

This dream was so long and involved I needed to make an outline before writing the dream: "bicycle 1, warehouse store, meeting, photo session, warehouse sports, bicycle 2, fences, warehouse/Sun God/sports, stockyard worm, fire truck, allies, fences/crows"

ANTHONY D. SINNER

Nightmare of the Evil Woman

I met an eccentric old woman who took me to her mansion. She was very wealthy, but the house was rather run-down with only a single servant to attend to it.

   She began to tell me the tale of her great obsession. We were in a windowless, cramped, basement-level bedroom. The bed was not made and the whole room was washed in the amber of the incandescent light. She proceeded to tell me how she would invite pre-teen girls to her home, girls she did not know, girls she just happened upon. She would bring them here and show them trinkets and purses and things. She then began to explain, "These are the knuckle-bones of a young girl and this bag is made from her skin."

   At that moment I witnessed in my mind that girl, beginning to realize her situation and starting to panic. I saw the old woman grab the girl and strangle her with the bedclothes. I was beyond horrified. I began to fear for my life.

   Somehow it became known to me that I would never leave this place, and I, like other young men she had brought here, would be held and used for some sinister reproductive purpose. I found myself alone in a basement bathroom. Someone came pounding violently at the door. I had no way out. I knew it was her. I went to he door to hold her off. I opened a small peep hole in the door and a sneering face was pressed up against the grating of the opening. It was not the old woman but an old college buddy, Harry. He was a captive, too.

The two of us experienced many harrowing adventures there trying to escape. Eventually, we did.

January 27, 2005

ANTHONY D. SINNER

Estate

I was visiting a large and wealthy estate. I was not a member of the family, nor did I have any financial stake in the estate, but I had been given permission to wander the grounds on my own. The landscape was lush and varied and beautifully maintained; the buildings stuccoed, clean and stately.

I experienced a sense of elation just being there. Everything was fabulous, expertly crafted, well organized, smartly upkept. Was there someone associated with this place who was important to me? A woman? I didn't know. I would explore.

After checking out a gift shop I entered a door ("A", see diagram). The door was tall and narrow with a pointed-arch top. It was made of highly polished natural wood, medium brown, and had a counterpart 15 feet away. The doors were maybe 25 feet tall. I wondered how one would install such a door and I came up with a satisfactory idea for how it could be safely hung on its massive hinges. It had to do with scaffolding that would keep the door from falling down while providing a way up for a worker to fasten the top hinge.

Once past the massive door I roamed through a large lobby and into a more intimate personal area. There was a very old man in a night shirt and cap walking about the darkened corridors, apparently preparing for bed. He tolerated me like he was resigned to tourist traffic or he had been fantasizing about an intruder who would someday show up to rob and kill him and put him out of his misery. I imagined he was a great uncle who shared the curse of the great wealth that held this grandiose domestic industry afloat. He grumbled in my direction as he passed me more than one time during his tired bedtime routine. I felt like I was encroaching on his personal space and moved on.

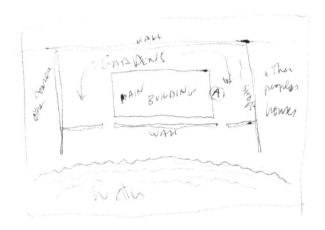

Later, I opened a door that led to a large theater. I entered on the balcony level, which held the only seating in the room. About ten feet below the balcony was a large rectangular stage floor covered with strange markings and moving images. I concluded that it was a hologram theater. Toward the front there were four vignettes which seemed to be playing in well-timed succession. The one currently playing was the second from the left, a dog show with a man and a woman and a couple of dogs, doing slick, but unspectacular tricks. I thought about the coordination of the acts and marveled at the colors and the lighting – and all in holograms, no less.

The balcony was filled, wall-to-wall, with beds covered in old patterned quilts. There were no aisles. One simply walked across the beds, oversized and edge to edge, and sat down. Other people were there, including an elderly woman with children.

As I got up to leave I saw a door a short distance from the one where I had entered. A woman was exiting that door. I quickly ran out my door and observed that there was no door where she should have been exiting and no one else in the hallway outside. There was something strange about this place. I walked down to where her door should have been and then, a little farther to a deeply-set, heavily-framed door. There was a square peephole. I looked in and saw the shrunken perspective of a peephole viewed from the wrong side. The room appeared dark with a tiny red light at the far end. I moved on.

I came to an area with windows to the outdoors. There was a rack on the wall with books about photography and graphic design. A little further on I entered another space, this one dark to the world and painted muted green, like a 1940s ad campaign. These looked like the offices of a marketing agency, differentiated spaces for design, production, lots of graphic materials all over, and hand-painted pop-art signs on office doors. The ceilings were maybe thirty feet high and it seemed like things had not been updated for decades. Many of the signs were written in Cyrillic characters. I felt like a tourist again, never really welcomed or acknowledged. So, I moved on.

dreamed 2/16/09 am

Pursued

First dream. There had been a competition, maybe a football game, which involved a play – not altogether fair – in which a hypodermic needle was used. It was not used like a hypodermic needle or syringe is commonly used, but more like a ball or a helmet would be used. And someone, a friend, recognized the unjust play, associated it with me and pursued me and the syringes through the school. I hid and collected and assembled the syringes into long segmented rods.

Later I had a different dream involving a blonde man with a scruffy beard and unkempt hair. He wore a white tank top under an unbuttoned blue-plaid, long-sleeved shirt. His face was without much shape or color, a rude construction without aesthetic value. I presumed he was an ex-convict. By the time I had remembered this dream I had forgotten how I met the man, but it was in my hometown and he had already shown his menacing face by the time the next dream began.

Next dream. I was at home, with my father, mother and a couple they knew. I was a middle-aged man, maybe fifty years old. During the course of banal social interactions I noticed someone outside our dining room window. I went to the window and saw him as he soberly tried to get my attention. It was the menacing man.

I opened the window to address him, separated now only by the insect screen. He said, with subtle irritation, "I'd like to talk to Mr. Russell." I told him, "There is no Mr. Russell here," and shut the window. His look said to me that he believed Mr. Russell was indeed inside the house and he didn't appreciate me trying to hide that fact. I had no idea who Mr. Russell was, but thought he must have mistaken my father for him. He slowly left the area, but seemed wholly unsatisfied.

Soon after, I went to the living room to look out the front of the house. Shockingly, a car had nosed up to within inches of the house, right under the picture window, literally threatening our home. The menacing man was in the driver's seat. The vehicle was a 1970s Dodge muscle car and looked like it was made of terra cotta, no chrome and matte finished all over, nothing shiny, not even the windshield. It pulsed slightly like the driver was on the brake and the gas, as if ready to smash through the front of the house. Apparently he thought he would have his Mr. Russell one way or another.

I ran to the phone while trying to alert the others in the house about the imminent danger. No one else seemed to have complete knowledge of the situation and had only casually noticed one thing or the other, never enough to recognize the true threat.

I tried to dial the phone, a cell phone, with little success. I tried to dial 9-1-1, but couldn't see well and ended up hitting an odd, non-number character instead of the nine. I tried repeatedly and finally successfully dialed, but was redirected to some non-emergency recording, cleverly substituted by the menace, I believed, to block all local emergency calls.

I made a run for it, leaving the house through the garage, rationalizing that someone must escape to save the others. When outside, I came across another scruffy man, similar in demeanor and appearance to the menace, but with a zipped jacket and an even more nondescript face. On a short, thick, black leash, he had a large black cat, one that scrambled continuously, apparently trying to free itself. The man held the leash high, making the cat struggle on two legs. I ran around him to get away and saw him fling a thing in my direction. I felt a light thud on my side.

I picked up the object and flung it back. It was a small piece of cooked chicken.

I began to run again, but was confounded by my heavy boots, their sticky laces tied together. I managed to quickly remove the boots, feeling success for the first time in the saga.

I ran down the street, scanning the houses for a house I knew, somewhere to ask for a phone. I came to a large group of people, apparently putting on a show or filming a movie. I didn't feel I could interrupt these people or that they could help me if I did. I kept on going. I saw other people watching the production. Many people were out in front of their houses, but I knew no one.

Saturday 6/19/10

Recalling the Horrible Event

My wife Mary and I were entertaining guests in our urban apartment. The apartment was not luxurious, but was on one of the top floors of a very tall building. It was decorated in a sleek, spare, sixties style; some vinyl, some avocado, nothing overstuffed.

I sat in the living room with our two guests, a man and a woman in their sixties. A married couple, they were the former caretakers of the apartment building. The horrible event had taken place several years earlier. The couple had discovered the aftermath of the horrible event, in which Mary's mother had perished.

The details of the event were well-known to us all. We had invited the caretaker couple to show them our appreciation for what they had so selflessly done to help Mary's mother, and to show our sympathy for the two of them, having endured involvement in the horrible event.

We were currently engaged in a cathartic recounting of the details of that fateful day. The gentleman sat in front of me, his wife to my side. He had been the one at the scene. She relived the events now as the supportive spouse. Mary was nearby, preparing drinks and food.

We retold the story with sadness and, by now, some chagrin. There was solace in his voice and a mild smile on his face as the caretaker relived the day. He had been accepted into the circle of Mary's family by the circumstances, circumstances that vaulted him over the protective inner wall of her family, where, otherwise, he could not have entered.

The caretaker knew what he saw that day, the moment written indelibly on his memory. But there were details that Mary's family had come to know later that the couple may not have known. I quizzed him. I asked him about two specific objects involved in the horrible event. One indistinct object resembled a dark garbage bag, albeit more solid. The other object was a two-handled spade. There was something sinister in these things, innocuous in themselves, of questionable utility, now filled with special meaning.

The caretaker was thinking hard to remember the objects in question, neither of us knowing if he had previous knowledge of them. He was keen to guess, if necessary, and wanted a chance to conjure the memory. At this moment, I stepped out to the adjoining bedroom, to blow my nose.

The tissue revealed blood. I looked in the mirror. I dabbed it. I looked closer, getting very near the mirror. There was blood, but not much. My nostril opened up. With the light reflecting off the mirror I could clearly see into the nasal cavity, easily daubing a brown mucous blob on the bridge side and some blood on the outer wall. I was able to reach in with my entire hand and tissue. It had never been so easy to remove unwanted stuff from inside my nose. My nostril was like a small room or closet and near the bridge side, or the left (it was my right nostril, reversed in the mirror), at the rear, was a door. It was a classic, white, six-panel door, apparently made of plastic. There was no casing around it, but blobs of blue glue could be seen around the frame, holding it in place. The blood was not flowing, just residual, so I turned from the mirror and headed back to our guests.

ANTHONY D. SINNER

When I returned the caretaker was still pondering. I wanted to relieve the suspense, but he wanted to keep on trying to divine, or recall, the objects of the horrible event.

dreamed 1/31/11

Tiny Chances

The pads that fit neatly into the inner sleeves of my football pants were missing. The game was imminent and I was becoming frantic. My search took me to many places in a large municipal building: a gymnasium, a ballroom, a stage, the bleachers. This venerable place was built for the ages with substantial woodwork, marble floors, and thick velvet curtains.

My search took me farther and farther, in mind and body, from anything related to football. Eventually I emerged outside with no athletic bag or equipment, upon steep, jagged, white cliffs far above a cool, churning ocean. As I surveyed my surroundings I saw a huge industrial complex in the distance, perched on the same tortuous cliffs which traced the shoreline here for miles. Nearer to me on a rocky point were large amorphous buildings overhanging the cliffs, supported by a vast framework of pipes, braces and scaffolding, colored in well worn hues of cream and bluish green.

The whole complex was comfortably separated from the building I had just exited, but they were certainly related in some way. The building I had just been searching through was square in floor plan, three stories high and very large. It had non-utilitarian windows, but was of similar color to the neighboring industrial site. I concluded that the building was for people – entertaining, convening, hobnobbing.

I began to move along the cliff edge to the web of pipes and scaffolding pinned precariously to the rocks below and the industrial complex above. Scrambling in and out on narrow,

ANTHONY D. SINNER

weathered catwalks and painted metal platforms, I passed myriad pieces of equipment hanging out over the sea. Most of it was unfamiliar and largely indescribable, consisting of troughs, spigots, tanks, funnels and piers.

I did recognize some safety equipment, paraphernalia demanded by code, I suppose, weathered by the sea air, probably never used. Specifically, I saw lifeboats, ostensibly to escape some calamitous event in the plant above by launching to the sea below. One boat, painted bluish green, was hanging bow-down from fifty feet above the water with an unsinkable flashlight carefully placed on the side of a seat. I imagined a good wind would easily dislodge the flashlight and therefore assumed the condition of the safety equipment was regularly checked.

Looking up at the complex I could see, through lighted windows, men talking and working at what appeared to be the control center of the great station. It seemed that I was where I should not be, but instead of ducking away to avoid detection, I decided to go up to the complex and try to enter. I fully expected to be escorted away, post-haste.

Climbing across framework, ducking my head, jumping across wide gaps, I eventually arrived at an oval metal door. This door was just a few levels below the window where I had spied the workers. I gingerly entered to find myself in an oval room with other closed doors and an oval-shaped opening leading to a lighted stairway. The stairs went up and so did I. Another oval room, another stairway, and I had arrived at what I imagined was the control center of the complex.

At the far end of this large room was another, smaller room visible through an open door. This smaller room looked like the helm of a great ship with windows all around looking out to the sea. Men in official hats moved around there doing official-looking things. In the warmly lit larger room where I was, one official was speaking with two women wearing heavy coats over night clothes. He appeared to be about to show them out as if a cordial, impromptu tour had just ended. It was almost as if this was the scene of a an alien abduction. The only incongruities were the pleasant demeanor of the players and their shared flesh and blood humanity.

The women turned to face me. The shorter one, maybe an inch or two over five feet, greeted me openly with a broad smile, teeth showing perceptible gaps. She was very lovely with her long, dark hair readied for bed. Her braless breasts swayed gently beneath her thin night gown with every turn of her head. Her taller, lighter-haired friend was also friendly, but did not draw my closer attention.

I sensed my time at the control center was at an end so I took the initiative to find my own way out. I turned and went down the stairs to the room I had initially entered. The incandescent glow of the room made the cream-colored walls very orange and the blue-green door almost brown. I looked out at the web of steel, now silhouetted against the twilight, but instead of going out the way I came I chose one of the other doors, hoping to go deeper into the catacombs of the complex. I opened the door and there was a stairway but it went up, not down as I had hoped. I went outside.

The air was pleasant. I took only a few steps on a short boardwalk before encountering the same lovely woman from the control room, now dressed and wearing a denim jacket and slacks. She was sitting on the worn wood, her friend a few yards away. She was charming.

We exchanged small greetings. As I looked at her I consciously decided to take the chance. Why not? So I said very honestly, "Would you like to make love to me?" The reply came softly, "But what about my boyfriend?"

Her words teetered on this cliff, not knowing which way to drop.

dreamed February 2011

ANTHONY D. SINNER

Top Secret Anti-Grav Car

Family, friends and relatives had gathered at my boyhood home for a late summer event. While casual dining and conversation took place indoors I had wandered to the backyard with an adult female companion.

We were in the southwest corner of our backyard when I saw an extraordinary thing. A car was floating through the clear air above the vacant lot beside our house. It did a few slow turns as if descending a whirlpool and landed lightly in the neighbor's back yard to the southwest.

The car had no wheels but was in every other way an automobile – a convertible in fact. It was white with squared-off edges like a 1980s boxy sedan. There were no wings but where the wheel wells would have been there were panels inserted (the seams could be seen). Two small oval-shaped grills were centered on each of these panels. In every other way it was an ordinary car, with windshield, headlights, front and back seats.

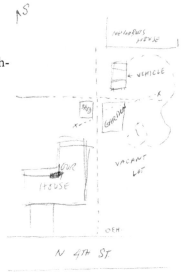

I had seen a car like this before, a flying car, but it had wheels. That other car was cosmetically indistinguishable from a regular car except that it could fly. It flew like this one did, with no jet engine or wings or tail. Both obviously operated on some new anti-gravity locomotion that was so secret nothing had ever been published about it. But I had seen it.

Since the vehicle I was witnessing today had no top I could see a driver and passenger during the flight and then again on the ground. When they got out of the car they seemed confident and happy to be alive, like a couple arriving at a country club. Then they turned and stood for a moment, admiring the vehicular marvel. With controlled enthusiasm they seemed to be discussing their recent flight. They were not, however, the people I knew to live in the neighbor's house.

I moved closer while staying in our yard, stretching to get a better look at the car. It had landed in a place that put a garden shed between it and us, partially obstructing my view. I crept to one corner of the shed while my companion slunk to the other. I didn't know what she had seen. She was looking at me in silent inquisition as we inched forward.

Just as I poked my head around the corner of the shed the car disappeared. It didn't drive away or fly away, it faded away, as if the driver had activated something remotely, like on a key fob lock. The secret would be safe now. The invisible, anti-gravity convertible could sit on our neighbor's back lawn undetected. Except that we had seen it.

Now I felt I must pull myself together. How long had I stood and stared? What had I really seen? That latter question was apparently on the mind of the man who now approached me. He was a fit, sandy-haired fellow with a medium build and a stone-cold expression. He walked up to me directly, not quickly or slowly – earnestly.

He wore an unusual lustrous suit. It was white with pearl-grey piping and a rich red emblem. The emblem, centered on his chest, was like an inverted ankh with the stem cut off and some other small details in the  middle. His short-cropped hair revealed a receding hairline, a hairline he would never care about. His unwavering blue eyes were fixed on me. I stood and waited for him to say something. I suspected what he was about.

This person and several others calmly escorted us back to our house and followed us inside. They said little and did not break a smile. Several of these agents, men and women, milled around in the front yard, guarding the door. It was clear these were federal agents following some protocol regarding the leak of ultra-sensitive government information. I knew now that I had seen too much.

I went to the door leading to the garage. Through the glass pane in the door I could see more agents there, talking, guarding, not noticing me. I began to feel a little claustrophobic, a little helpless, a little desperate. I went down the hall to the bathroom and checked the window. More of them outside. I wondered how the situation would ultimately be resolved. I waited.

dreamed early April, 2011

Reuben and the Corporate Headquarters

Reuben came to dinner. Reuben was a Benedictine monk and sculptor who taught at St. Luke's University beginning in the1960s. I would have thought he would be impossibly old or deceased by this time but he was indeed alive and willing to show up as our guest. There was some question as to his state of mind and we anticipated the need to treat him gently.

After eating, Reuben, Mary and I left our home and went for a walk around the city. We came to a religious building and I was explaining that I liked the architecture but not the

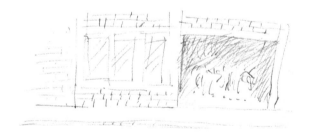

religious elements. I was trying to make sure Reuben understood that I was by this time an atheist. He was oblivious to any of these social cues and went on and on about the catholic symbols and paraphernalia in the deep, low, street-side courtyard. It was filled with handsome stonework, reliquaries and gravestones.

Later, we took him to a Parisian district I had been to

several times before. It was an area set up to show how the people of Paris lived, starting in the middle ages. We traveled a road that looped around the periphery of the area. This place was like an historical reenactment exhibit, the beginning showing the oldest times, and moving along to ultimately reach the modern era. The exhibits consisted of racks and racks of rustic commodities like straw, sheaves of grain, coarse cloth and sticks. It was adjacent to a similar space that appeared to be a market. Reuben prattled on unconsciously about the middle ages and a little bit about the things in front of us, but he was not very impressed with any of it.

In the end we returned to modern civilization, ending up in a large corporate office building. The three of us wandered around there for some time, riding elevators that always seemed to open on the floor we had just been on. Eventually, Mary and I found ourselves in a small auditorium. When entering I had noticed a series of deep, square niches set in the azure-colored wall above the door we entered. In each of the half-dozen or so niches sat a woman I knew from college. These women were recognizable in that they retained their former shapes and colors, but were, upon closer inspection, noticeably aged. They appeared to be important, experienced workers or executives, dressed in snappy business clothes, sitting in office chairs and full of attentive energy. They all looked in the direction of the dais at the front of the room. Behind the dais were more occupied niches above a wall of windows revealing the bright light and green hues of a beautiful tree-filled summer day.

On the stage, two thirty-somethings with bold brown-framed glasses gave a casual and confident preamble to the meeting. Mary and I had found firm, stylish, plywood and metal chairs to perch on. By this time, however, Reuben was off on his own, presumably still on the premises. The young presiding gentlemen listened to a report from someone in one of the niches. After a short back and forth it was discovered that the budget for a particular item to be given to all workers was double the expected amount. Quickly and calmly, one of the gentlemen suggested that everybody write off the extra twenty dollars as "software." And on they went.

We found a convenient moment to leave and reentered the large room we had come in from, which was full of people and cubicles and business activity. Soon we saw Reuben running through a door at the far end of the room, chased by corporate men, perhaps security. We heard the commotion as they left the room, surmising that they had gone up one level. Feeling responsible for him, Mary and I darted for the elevator near us.

This elevator functioned as the others had throughout the day. It opened where it had begun. Thinking about this I concluded that we were in an ultra-modern office building, one in which the elevators themselves did not move. When you closed the doors and pressed a button, the entire floor would move up or down in the building. Brilliant!

Trying to rescue Reuben now became more confusing. Much later I asked him why he had run. He explained to me that he could tell by the look of the men approaching him that he had no choice but to run. Presently though, I was just trying to find a way out. To another elevator in the corner...too small. I began to follow exit signs. Now I was passing throngs of corporate workers, some in dance groups, all seeming to wear things that suggested "clown." Increasingly they were acting happy, greeting me as they mimed and danced as if in a stage show.

I escaped to an open, darkened area like a convention hall. On the wood floor in front of a large television was a creature or automaton – I'm not sure which. He, or it, consisted of a dress shoe and one pinstripe pant leg curled over a hidden head, frightened eyes peering from beneath a fold in the fabric. Pants Man seemed scared and annoyed and tried to ignore me. I

ANTHONY D. SINNER

continued to follow exit signs and
saw one on a door in the floor. It was
too small for me to go through so I
grabbed Pants Man and stuffed him,
eyes now tightly shut, through the
door in the floor.

Immediately a giant eel creature burst out of the floor
door and latched onto my hand. Its bite was firm but not painful.
I pushed it off and began to run but it just kept coming, yards
and yards of fat eel creature flying through the air. Then another
eel just the same burst out, and then another smaller one. They
caught me and I stopped to fight them off. I grabbed all three
and, pushing them to the floor with my two fists, popped them
like plastic bags.

Vanquished, flattened and lifeless, they sprawled across
the floor like wide, brown seaweed.

*dreamed on or about June 30, 2011 at Cedar Shores Resort, Park
Rapids, Minnesota, written July 5, many elements of this long and
complex dream were too indistinct to record*

Worm Hole

A group of us was traveling in three vans across the rural countryside. It was daytime. Included among us was Mary, my wife, cousin Peter, boyhood friend Jack, and many others, totaling about twenty. I assumed my parents were in the leading van, our family vehicle from the 1970s, a two-toned tan Chevy.

After some time travelling the vans were still in close contact, trundling down a gravel road. I was in the second van and our view of the lead van was often obscured by a bend in the road or by dust kicked up by tires on the dry surface. Suddenly, we came upon construction workers, warning signs, and municipal vehicles stopping our progress. The road ahead had simply disappeared into water. And there was no van ahead of us now.

There must have been some localized flooding as the road just descended a few feet and entered a large pond. I jumped out and asked if anyone had seen another van come this way. No one had seen one. I knew intuitively that, since I had last seen the lead van, there had been no other possible egress. It must have gone this way. It should be right in front of us, waiting like we were. Where was it?

I looked intently at the water. Just past the spot where gravel met pond, I could make out something submerged. It was dark and very large…a railroad car. If the van had gone in, it would be sitting there, right there. The water was shallow enough to see that there was no vehicle under the water there, just a derelict freight car, probably decades in that spot. And the workers had obviously been there for some time, long enough to

ANTHONY D. SINNER

set up signs and barriers. They had seen nothing.

We got our van turned around and eventually made it to a nearby farm site where we were kindly invited into the house while we tried to sort things out. We gathered in a long room at one end of the large home, with a brown-speckled linoleum floor, dark woodwork and glass block features. A large window looked out to an expansive lawn and farmyard.

I asked everyone about the missing van, what they had seen, what explanation they had. Mary and Peter were here. I went outside briefly to walk and think. While outside I witnessed the most astounding sight of my life. In the sky above the clouds, stretching from horizon to horizon, was an enormous space ship. Owing to its size and the current cloud cover, I could only see parts of it at any one time. It was an assemblage of massive components of different shapes and sizes, purplish blue parts silhouetted against the afternoon sky. I calculated its size to be some large fraction of the earth's itself. It moved only just perceptibly across my world.

Soon I returned to the farmhouse room. I began to formulate a theory regarding the missing van. I suspected a worm-hole. People around me were talking about the value of the missing van and insurance claims. I smiled and told them how old the van was and that its value was only about $200. But I continued to think about the worm-hole idea: the idea that things can be swallowed up and instantly transported to another place and time.

It was now dusk and the view out the window showed a thick layer of winter snow and a faint glow of electric blue. The glow was coming from just below the window. I put my head against the window to try and see. The glow radiated from a conspicuous funnel of new snow descending, it seemed, into a basement window well just below the large window. I could not quite see to the bottom of the funnel.

I looked up only to see the enormous spaceship again, covering the sky, slowly moving. As I called my friends to come and see this most astounding of sights I began to fit pieces of the day's puzzle together: the worm-hole was at the base of the funnel; the wormhole radiated strange electromagnetic energy that caused hallucinations in people close to it; the spaceship was one of these hallucinations.

I ran outside to get a better look. The deep snow made it difficult to move. As I circled around the funnel I still could not get close enough to see the bottom of it. The blue light continued to glow. Suddenly, people began to emerge from the worm-hole, the people from the missing van. Jack was the first to emerge. I tried to explain where they had been and how they had disappeared and now returned. Jack would have none of it, giving some mundane alternative explanation of their apparent travels through space-time. I concluded that the worm-hole energy had protected them with familiar hallucinations.

As more people emerged and I saw all were safe, I asked about the van itself. Someone produced, in hand, a tiny model van to prove its existence. I looked carefully at this Matchbox-sized vehicle. It was a van. It was two-tone tan, but it was a different make and model than our van.

dreamed July 29, 2011, written August 1

ANTHONY D. SINNER

Bernie's Medical Issue

My brother Bernie and I were going to a local play field to play catch. We were adults. The way to the field was through a series of back yards. We wound in and out around houses, along sidewalks, always in someone's backyard, never crossing a street or seeing the front of a house. I noticed that Bernie had a ball in his hand, swinging it back and forth as we jogged. It was a small, yellow, plastic football, like a booster-club-handout football. Of all the balls he could have brought, I wondered why he was bringing *that* ball.

The day produced light so even and colors so vivid it was like overcast twilight. At one point we heard a dog barking and Bernie nimbly tacked to the right to avoid that yard. Pretty soon Bernie was running, shirtless, ahead of me, up a grassy incline. It was at this point that I saw what looked like a long loop of thick, brown rope trailing behind him. It was attached at his waistline. I ran a little faster to catch up and see what it was. It was a long section of his intestines that had somehow breached his abdominal wall on his right side. When I stopped him he realized what was wrong and dropped to the ground. Suddenly he seemed to feel intense pain and began to writhe on the ground.

We had just reached the play field when Bernie collapsed so I ran to a nearby park building where there was a phone. The phone was like a utility box with a plastic, molded cover. I opened it and began to dial. I pushed "9" but could not find a "1". There were only 3 or four numbers and no "1". I saw an alternate keypad but the buttons were so small I could not see the numbers nor even fit my finger on just one at a time. I opened a small door that revealed to a third set of push buttons. This pad was foam rubber and the numbers to push were the high points in what looked like a field of frozen interference waves. But there was no indication of numbers, just raised areas.

I gave up and began to search for help. I could see Bernie still writhing but more quietly now. There was a uniformed EMT a few yards away talking to someone. I interrupted him and yelled, "We have a medical emergency, here!" He calmly began to assess the situation.

dreamed the week of August 11, 2014

ANTHONY D. SINNER

Hugo and the Silver Sliver

Imagining that Hugo had fallen dead, alone in a dark corner of his studio, a jarring sense of foreboding came over me. The venerable academic was very likely near the end of his days. He was a painter and print-maker who, long ago, had tried to teach me that there is a prescribed path any respectable artist should follow. Now, having long forgotten his vain efforts to mentor me, he lived his last days – or years – working.

I peered into the unlit space, the darkness confounding me. Was that him there, akimbo on the floor? As my eyes adjusted I could see he was there, slumped...but not dead. He was apparently masturbating under his smock. I left before he noticed me. He was not noticing much at that moment.

Later I came back to find him working with a model. She was pale, nude, and laid flat as a plank with a decorative cardboard screen casually hiding a dark mons veneris. I saw his strategy now: to remove the sexual distraction before she arrived by arranging the room this way. At this point in his life time was the most valuable of all commodities.

I slid casually by, acting as if the spread of flesh was nothing to me. But it *was* something...something to respect with a cool dignity. She returned the gesture.

I arrived at my work area, a very different space from Hugo's. Not well-defined in purpose, not well-lit, not well-equipped. My work was also different. Hugo was a practiced hand; movements rehearsed and owned, ethic established, pattern professed, mantra droned daily.

I began to begin to work. I took stock and stood back. There was a thing distracting me. It was my finger…the middle finger on my left hand…the pad at the end…the top of the pad…a problem…a pain.

I remembered. I got something in there, like a thorn. I looked and touched and found the tiny spot. I magnified it. Closer. Then closer still. The texture of my skin was geometric, rectangular ridges of skin riddled with black flecks. And then I saw it: the tell-tale glint of the shiny silver end of the offending object, a thing self-embedded in some hasty action a couple of days before.

I squeezed the pad to try to produce an expulsive pressure. I jabbed at the skin around the tiny poking end with a tweezer, trying to find a surface to grip. It began to move upward. It levitated. It startled me the way it moved, as if it was a charmed snake. It was indeed silvery. And long and thick. It appeared to be a rolled length of tin foil, tinted with life's blood, faceted and glinting.

Another thing emerged from the tiny wound. It was a shiny silver ball bearing, popping out like a baby's head. Then another ball bearing just the same. I laid the three objects on the table. The rolled-up tin foil was roughly the size and shape of a large human finger; each ball bearing an inch in diameter. This struck me as odd.

Hugo had taken a break by now. I showed him the silvery things that had come out of my finger. I showed them with smiley pride. He had maybe seen such a thing before but more likely he had stopped caring about astonishing things in favor of his work, which he knew for sure and seemed to regard as reality itself. I looked at the silvery, genital group, glazed in afterbirth on the table at the dark end of the room. The objects glinted with pride.

Hugo's model was there again. But before he began to work at the well-lit end of the room, he pulled down a short stack of papers from a white cupboard above the counter in his studio.

The papers were mostly half sheets, copied from typewritten originals, expositions on academic art, like mixing oil paints, etc. He told me to take them and use them, they were now mine. Among these papers were other small scraps and cards, advertisements and signs, some modern. He said that he was told not to use the "Dora the Explorer" ones (presumably for copyright reasons). He admonished me to also heed this advice.

dreamed and written 12/16/16

The Extraterrestrial Agenda

A spate of dreams: I dreamed about spending quality time with the President and First Lady, Barrack and Michelle Obama, then engaged in some non-golf activity (possibly food-related) on a steep embankment near a large body of water with professional golfer, Phil Mickelson, and later discussed lyrics with music icon, Cat Stevens. In subsequent dreams I name-dropped the Obamas several times, including during a party at my house, where I also accidentally sprayed soda on a table of colorfully-clad Caribbean revelers. I had come to the party after exiting a car in protest over the Indian driver who was not fully on board with the agenda of the extraterrestrials who had modified the vehicle to include advanced technologies and controls that allowed it to fly and teleport. The extraterrestrials had even provided low-tech fake IDs for those of us who *were* on board with their agenda. I was getting the driver up to speed on the features of the car – which I had been trained in on in a dream somewhere between spending time with the Obamas and hosting the party – when the driver became intransigent.

❀

5/28/19, didn't sleep well due to a sore toe

Lucid

I found myself in a school building walking a narrow path between an array of school desks on my left and a row of lockers on my right. As I walked I observed the floor immediately at my feet, step by intentional step. Low-angle light made the checkered, soft-colored linoleum a thing of beauty.

Occasionally, I looked up at the doorway ahead of me which was open to the outdoors. A fleeting shadow darkened the doorway briefly but the related figure never appeared. Now I was dreaming lucidly, expecting a figure to show itself, prompting a figure to appear. It did not.

Some time later I was with my sons in a pavilion with some summertime food choices and a smattering of familiar people. Jude was a young boy, maybe eight years old. He was affectionate and nuzzley and open. I began to realize his true real-life self was much older. I asked him how old he was. He said, "twelve." I then explained to him that this was really a dream and he was actually nineteen now. He was as unimpressed as he could be.

He noticed a van just outside the pavilion with its back open and a man selling things out of it. We knew this vendor from previous years' visits here. He wanted to go see if the blonde-headed, muscle-shirted, side-burned vendor had the bags of used golf balls he usually did. Impulse told me to recommend against it. Did Jude really need more golf balls? Did he have any money? Blah, blah.

Remembering that this was actually a dream I instead conspired with him to make an extravagant purchase. I took out my wallet and explained to the young Jude that we could go ahead and spend the money without consequence. However, as I leafed through the bills I began to doubt just a little that the scene playing out was actually happening in dreamland. So I gave Jude my most doubtful bills, an eighteen-dollar bill and a zero-dollar bill. There were other design features that made this currency look more like travelers checks than paper money, but I sent Jude off to have his fun, regardless.

Next I saw Jude's older brother, Barrett, and wanted to let him in on the dream. I sat in a grassy spot near him. He moved away a little, behind a clear, inflatable mound. I could see his distorted shape through the bubble-like cells of the mound. There were cobwebs on the outside of it and I could see a large spider. I motioned to Barry to come nearer and he inadvertently touched the spider as he made his way around the mound. I explained to him that he was actually twenty-one, not fourteen as he thought he was (he seemed more like ten) and that our time together here was actually a dream. I told him of the things he had done in his college years and how proud we were of him. I became tearful.

dreamed and written 6/9/19

ANTHONY D. SINNER

Soccer Balls

I was playing soccer indoors – two on two with goalies. The ball went over the end line, last touched by one of my opponents. Nobody, including me, knew the long-standing corner kick rule which governed such situations. So, I played the ball in with my foot near the end line on the left side. I sent a careful pass to my teammate and moved toward the goal. I needed to strike the ball very carefully because it was an egg, about the size of an egg a duck might lay. As I approached the goal my teammate let go a nice shot which the goalie deflected downward. It bounced up in front of me and I headed it into the back of the net for a goal. The ball was still an egg. It did not break.

Later we moved to a training area with four balls to use. The balls were neatly folded clothes. Each ball was either a neatly folded silk shirt or neatly folded genie pants. Whenever we started to play, the ball quickly became undone and, frustratingly, unplayable. I got the brilliant idea of a Velcro strap arrangement that could keep the folded-clothes balls from coming unfolded so quickly. I thought it could possibly turn out be a money maker.

10/8/19

The Running of the Beasts

Mary moved purposefully along the slope of the rocky hill. She was very small from my vantage point across the valley, but unmistakable nevertheless. It was not unusual for her to strike out on her own if no one else was interested in her excursive idea. I decided to set out across the valley to join her.

The looming mount was etched with switchbacks on its upper slopes, its lower third a sheer rock wall giving way to a pastoral foundation. This expansive green rose to my left, eventually swallowing up the rock face and making contact with the upper slopes. As I got closer I could see that the switchbacks – essentially one long winding trail – were so vertically compressed that a trail traversing hundreds of yards laterally rose only a few feet up the slope. Practically speaking, a hiker could simply take a giant step straight up or down the slope and reach the next leg of the trail.

Mary had made her way back down to the grassy area fronting the rock wall by the time I arrived there. Other people had gathered there too, lining up along as if in anticipation of some event. Reports of an angry bull (apparently soon expected) spread throughout the crowd. I began to worry about this, thinking we had stumbled into some local ritual for which we were unprepared.

I stepped forward away from the crowd just as a raging bull and rider came charging from my right. I started, stumbled and fell directly into its path. I rolled frantically back toward the crowd, barley avoiding the charging bull. It glared at me as

ANTHONY D. SINNER

it passed at full speed, seemingly frustrated to have missed his chance to gore me. The rider rode with enthusiasm. The crowd cheered.

Mary and I began to piece together our situation. The ritual, the game, the contest went something like this: a contestant must bring three animals down the mountain, one by one, in succession, starting with the animal whose name started with the letter nearest the beginning of the alphabet. The second animal's name must start with the next letter of the alphabet, and the third, the next letter. So if the first animal a contestant brought down the mountain was a bull, the second must be a cougar or a crab or a cod, etc. The third, a dingo or a dormouse or a dove, etc. When a contestant had successfully brought the third animal down the mountain they had completed their turn. The only other animals I had seen to this point were bees.

We quickly moved away from the hill, anticipating the arrival of additional dangerous animals. We left the mass of onlookers and were able to scramble up a lone tree fifty yards clear of the event. The tree's sprawling branches wobbled and swung as we braced ourselves, as if hunkering down for a hurricane. As the sky darkened I noticed an eerie blue light illuminating us from a distant low source. I was distracted for a moment by the cinematic beauty of us clinging to the spooky, swaying tree. Mary didn't seem to care about how beautifully cinematic it all was.

The sky brightened and the danger seemed to have passed and we came down from our perch. A smug young man approached and accosted me, telling me I had been chosen to bring down a trio of beasts from the mountain. A compatriot of his was preparing a satchel of bees, presumably as my first run. I was determined to find some way to politely refuse my nomination. The recruiter sensed my discomfort and offered me a way out ... the sixty years and older rule.

dreamed 1/16/20, written 1/19/20, at age 59 1/2

Printed in the USA
CPSIA information can be obtained
at www.ICGtesting.com
CBHW051116081124
17082CB00021B/541